To George,

Thanks for
thinking about
Maine!

TABLE OF CONTENTS

A FOREWORD BY SENATOR ANGUS KING

In 1835, a farmer in North Berwick, Maine named William Hussey created a new design for a plow blade. It was more efficient, easier to use, and more durable than what had come before and soon it became the international standard in what was then a huge market. Hussey built a factory in his hometown and manufactured his state-of-the art plows, refining the design for the next sixty years. That's innovation.

But in the early morning hours of January 11, 1895, a fire swept through the factory, all but destroying the business. William Hussey's grandsons decided not only to rebuild, but also to refocus the business on other types of steel fabrication—like fire escapes and bridge supports--to meet new market demands. That's optimism, resilience and re-invention.

Then in 1931, a next generation Hussey who was working on a project for the Portland Boys Club conceived a design incorporating steel and wood into a new kind of outdoor bleacher—and he later adapted the design for use indoors. And the business was re-invented once again.

Over the next 85 years, came more innovation and re-invention— the telescoping gym bleachers we all remember from high school, higher-end folding chair seating for civic centers around the world (there are now more than a million installed), polymer stadium seats and upholstered auditorium seats, and even throw-back classic seats for the newest vintage-look baseball stadiums.

I believe the story of Hussey Seating tells you all you need to know about the elements of success in the next economy: innovation, re-invention, resilience, optimism, and the ability to adapt to new and changing markets. The only difference is that the transformations which took decades a century ago can and must take years (or more likely months or weeks) today.

So how about a new motto for Maine, to go along with "I lead"? My proposal is "I ROAR" (Innovation, Re-invention, Optimism, Adaptation, Resilience)? Kind of a fun idea.

In the pages that follow, Alan Caron and his co-authors lay out the case for a bright future for Maine based upon these principles--and provide strategies for getting there. As I have learned, and as they emphasize, there is no silver bullet, no one policy change or tactic which will propel us forward, but instead, there are many interrelated pieces which taken as a whole will allow and encourage the innovation and continuous re-invention necessary for success in this new century.

This does not mean the abandonment of our traditional industries; paper and wood products, boat building, fishing (including aquaculture), farming (which is already undergoing a new birth), and the manufacturing of everything from salt shakers to jet engine parts will all be important to Maine's future. But so will software, tourism, back office services, design, advertising, bio-tech, new kinds of manufacturing (3-D printing, anyone?) and hundreds of new businesses we can't even imagine. Who would have thought 30 years ago, for example, that a company making test kits for animal diseases would become one of Maine's largest employers?

I believe that for once, we have the wind at our back; for the first time in human history, people can work where they live rather than having to live where they work. And given the choice, who wouldn't want to live in a place like Maine? As long as we maintain the quality of place that is our most important calling-card, along with the infrastructure of growth (from transportation to broadband to education), we are in the hunt. It won't

IDEXX MAINE HEADQUARTERS

be easy—change never is, and the global competition is fierce—but given our array of talent and this fabulous place, I like our chances.

This book does not contain all the answers (if anybody has them all, please let me know), but it starts an important conversation between and among Maine business people, educators, policy-makers and engaged citizens on our 21st century destination and how to get there. I suggest we take a tip from seven generation of Husseys—and get started with a loud ROAR!

Angus King

Brunswick, Fall of 2015

THE AUTHORS

For the people who have filled these pages with their ideas and hopes, this book is a labor of love for Maine. It is our contribution to a long-overdue conversation about Maine's future, and how Mainers can create a new prosperity, shared by everyone.

We don't all agree with every word written here. But we do agree with the main themes of this book, which are that Maine has to look to the future, rely upon our capacity for innovation, and build the next economy from the bottom up.

Each of the contributing authors will be introduced as they appear in this book, at the end of their chapter. Let's start with the main author and primary orchestrator of this book.

 **Alan Caron** is a lifelong Mainer, raised in Waterville in a family of mill workers and farmers, who now resides in Freeport with his wife and son. He has been a small business owner and social entrepreneur for most of his life, working on issues ranging from growing businesses to revitalizing neighborhoods, affordable housing, solar energy, transportation, the environment and telecommunications.

He has also owned Caron Communications since 1987, advising business leaders, managers, and non-profits in Maine. He is the founder and President of Envision Maine, which works to promote Maine's next economy. Previously, Alan founded GrowSmart Maine, where he was responsible for bringing the Brookings Institution to Maine in 2006 to produce an influential report called *Charting Maine's Future*. In 2010 he co-authored *Reinventing Maine Government*, detailing how spending on Maine's government compares to other rural states and the nation.

He writes a weekly column for newspapers in Portland, Augusta, and Waterville, on topics ranging from the economy to politics to sports and life in Maine. He holds a Master's Degree in Public Administration from the Kennedy School of Government at Harvard University.

He can be reached at alancaroninmaine@gmail.com.

THANKS TO EVERYONE WHO HELPED

We are enormously grateful to the many people who have helped inspire and shape this book, whose work and enthusiasm have propelled it forward, and whose wisdom and encouragement have kept it alive. The list of people who have played an important role in this book is too lengthy to adequately cover, but we are particularly grateful to Dick Woodbury and Sam Fratoni, for their encouragement to finish this book. Thanks also to Eliot Cutler, for his early support. To Kristina Egan, for her commentary and confidence that it would get done. To Sarah Collins and John Lovell for their editing and eye for detail, and to Nathan Broaddus for his help with writing and design.

Above all, we need to thank the hundreds of people who have participated in meetings and discussions sponsored by Envision Maine over the last few years, and whose voices and ideas have found their way into this book.

All proceeds from this book, beyond the cost to produce it, will be dedicated to Envision Maine, a grassroots nonprofit organization that you can learn more about at www.envisionmaine.org.

THE PEOPLE WHO INSPIRED THIS BOOK

There are many pioneers of Maine's next economy who inspired us to write this book. All seem to share a belief in Maine's great potential and in the skill, resourcefulness, and goodness of Maine people.

Each of them took risks to build the future, in their own way and in their time. They sometimes failed, but always managed to get up and try again. None feared trying new approaches or charting a new course for themselves and for Maine. In the end, they seem to share one characteristic above all else, which is an incurable optimism about this state.

While we could include hundreds of similar examples, here are the 10 who we want to recognize as among the leading pioneers of Maine's next economy.

LEON L. BEAN

Maine's iconic entrepreneur took something that we don't grow – rubber – and used it to produce a boot that would keep people's feet dry in the wettest conditions. From the first boots sold out of Leon Leonwood Bean's brother's basement in 1912 to more than 100 factory and outlet stores in three countries today, L. L. Bean has embodied persistence, entrepreneurial spirit, and community engagement. Though its catalog and the main Freeport store initially accounted for most of the company's sales, it has flourished in the online sales era.

HAROLD ALFOND

In 1939, Harold Alfond purchased an abandoned shoe factory with his father and set off on a groundbreaking path in manufacturing, retail, and philanthropy. Taking the Maine habit for self-reliance into the business of manufacturing, Alfond's Dexter Shoe

Company was one of the first companies to both manufacture and retail its products, which began in Maine in 1971 and later extended throughout the country to 80 other factory outlet locations.

TOM AND KATE CHAPPELL

Tom and Kate Chappell took the idea of all-natural personal care products and blended them with Maine's reputation for quality and wholesomeness to build a company that was worth well over $100 million in 2006. Founded in 1970, Tom's of Maine is built on the idea that values have a place at the center of for-profit enterprise.

ROXANNE QUIMBY

Roxanne Quimby took another simple starting ingredient, beeswax, and moved from candles at a local crafts fair to a national brand that, again, fit Maine perfectly. Her company was worth well over $100 million by 2003 and many times that a few years later. Roxanne built Burt's Bees from $20,000 in sales in its first year to over half a billion dollars by the time it was sold to Clorox 23 years later in 2007.

JONATHAN KING AND JIM STOTT

Jonathan and Jim took their homemade jam from a farmers' market in southern Maine to a line of world-class products that, again, enhanced the Maine brand while benefiting from it. With little prior experience in business development but with a creative spark and a well-developed entrepreneurial spirit, Stonewall Kitchen has grown from simple beginnings as a farm stand vendor to a company with hundreds of employees, 10 retail stores, a cooking school, and more than 6,000 wholesale accounts.

BUZZ FITZGERALD

Buzz Fitzgerald rose from humble beginnings to become the CEO of BIW and a friend to both powerful and powerless people everywhere. No matter how far he climbed, Buzz never lost touch with his roots or forgot about the workers at BIW. Committed to fairness and integrity, Fitzgerald practiced law for 23 years before becoming the executive vice president of Bath Iron Works in 1987, quickly moving up to become the president and CEO only four years later.

RUSSELL LIBBY

Russell Libby not only inspired the growth of organic farming in Maine through the Maine Organic Farmers and Gardeners Association, but also pointed the way to the next economy by emphasizing small decentralized farming, trying new approaches to old problems, and building community.

Libby helped to guide MOFGA into becoming the largest organic farming organization in the country, with more than 6,500 members, 418 organic farms and food processors, and an education center operating year-round on more than 250 acres in Unity, Maine.

The recent resurgence of local food and small-scale farming in Maine can be largely attributed to Russell Libby's life's work.

RON PHILLIPS

Ron Phillips has been a tireless advocate for rural development and economic justice in Maine since the 1970s, when he established Coastal Enterprises. From its first steps as a three-person team, CEI has grown to employ 88 staff and now manages more than $980 million in capital investment. It has become a regional and national force for sustainable economic growth and justice.

A CONVERSATION ABOUT MAINE'S FUTURE
Alan Caron

This book is for optimistic people who love Maine, are action-oriented and determined to build a brighter future for themselves and their neighbors. It's about creating an economy that is driven by innovators, entrepreneurs and small businesses and that makes sense for Maine.

This is a celebration of Maine's doers: the inventors, entrepreneurs, risk-takers, artists, and small-business people who are hard at work, every day, laying the foundations of the next economy. They are the engines of change in Maine, and our best hope for the future.

Take a look around you and you'll see these folks in every community, in families, organizations, and companies. If you're reading these pages, you're probably one of them.

Maine's next economy is growing throughout the state. If we help it along, Maine can become a fertile place for small businesses to grow and a magnet for innovators from around the country and the world.

To get there, we need a big conversation about how we can create the kind of future we want and need. That's one goal of this book: to spark a discussion about where we're headed and how we can grow a more sustainable and widespread prosperity.

None of us has a crystal ball into the future. And imagining Maine's next economy has nothing to do with picking winners and losers over the next few years. What we have tried to do here is simply to share with you what we see happening today, the trends and opportunities and challenges that are arising, and where all of that could take us, if we work at it.

For many people, the idea of an innovation-driven economy in Maine may seem to be something new. But to those who appreciate Maine's history, it is really a rediscovery of some of our oldest and most successful traditions. Our past is full of tenacious innovators and resourceful, determined and hardy risk-taking characters.

In the pages ahead, you'll see how they confronted a rapidly changing world, in their time, and managed to not only survive, but also to prosper. They were able to do that because being innovators and entrepreneurs is part of our DNA. We're one of the birthplaces of Yankee ingenuity. We know how to 'make do' with what we have and to get the most out of it.

We'll introduce you to some of those inventors, dreamers and entrepreneurs, who were among the pioneers of Maine's next economy. And to a cross-section of current Maine companies – some old and some just now sprouting – that are on the leading edge of the next economy. We also look at how our economy has been changing over the last few decades, in ways that have been both profound and unsettling. And then peer into the next chapter of Maine's history, which is just now being written.

You'll see how Maine's economy has risen and fallen many times, and how in our time it's mostly fallen. For nearly two generation now, we've been stuck in what can only be called a long and painful recession. We've lost jobs, seen too many of our kids leave, and watched the state grow older.

Many people have begun to lose hope that Maine can adapt itself to the 21st century and build a new prosperity. Some have succumbed to anger and frustration and seem to fill their days with a search for scapegoats.

But others have been hard at work building the foundations of the next economy, and they're just now beginning to raise its walls.

In the final section of this book, we offer a basic plan for accelerating the growth of Maine's Next Economy. It has been shaped by a wide array of talented and thoughtful entrepreneurs and business people, public policy specialists, politicians, educators, nonprofit leaders, and others from across the state.

Some of that plan is about the things that every state needs to do to sustain a healthy economy, including providing good schools, roads, and Internet connections, safe communities, and dependable regulations. Those things are the price of admission to the modern economic table. But they are not, by themselves, a plan for growing our economy or differentiating ourselves from other places.

Part of the plan focuses on what you and other Maine's citizens can do, through individual initiative and by working together, to create the future we want. The remainder of it is about the role that government can play in partnering with Maine's innovators and entrepreneurs.

For our next economy to arise, and for Maine people to find a new prosperity in this state, we need to begin by confronting some difficult – and even unwelcome – realities.

1. Yesterday's jobs are not returning.

2. The next economy will not look like the old one. It will not be largely based on extracting natural resources or exporting bulk

commodities. We'll continue to have important jobs in natural resources, and many new ones are just now being created, but there will not be as many people working in those fields as in the past.

3. We're not going to attract jobs from away as much as grow them here.

4. More of tomorrow's jobs will be ones that we've created, rather than ones we apply for.

5. Government support for economic growth has to shift from trying to attract big companies to Maine to helping thousands of small startups, innovators, and entrepreneurs who are already here, or would come here if we create a supportive environment for them.

6. We can't improve our prosperity by circulating the same dollars around and around. We're going to need to grow things and make things that we can sell to the world, and in that way bring more resources into the state.

7. We'll need to greatly expand our technical skills and training, including in how to build businesses.

8. Tourism will continue to be a major part of our economy, but it too will need to reinvent itself and think in new ways.

There are a few things you won't find in these pages. One is lots of charts and graphs and technical data about the economy (there are a few). This is not a homework assignment or a college course. It's a way for the doers of Maine to see themselves in a larger picture, be engaged in a big conversation about Maine's future, and connect with others like them.

You also won't find a lot of hand-wringing about how beset we are with problems. There's more than enough of that elsewhere. We don't ignore Maine's problems, but we try to keep them in perspective.

A new economy has been quietly growing in Maine over this last decade, particularly in farming, renewable energy, and technology, and now spreading to other sectors. It's happening because growing numbers of Mainers have stopped waiting for yesterday's jobs to return. They don't expect a big company to parachute into Maine and provide jobs to everyone. And while they'd like more support from Augusta and Washington, they know that, in the end, they must build the future themselves, with support from each other, from the ground up.

There's a question often heard in Maine that seems to have appeared throughout our history whenever we have been confronted with a new set of challenges. It's a question that every innovative pioneer, entrepreneur, and successful company in Maine has asked, and that animates this book. The question is: "What are we going to do about it?" Mainers are doers. And across the state they're busy writing the next chapter of Maine's story. This book is about writing that chapter with the ending we want and need. It's about creating Maine's next economy by taking matters into our own hands, with each of us doing our part, and by working together.

That's the Maine way.

GROWING A NEW PROSPERITY IN MAINE

THE ECONOMY IS EVERYONE'S JOB

Most people live here for a reason. Some were born in Maine and refuse to leave. Others were attracted to the place by childhood visits, summers at camp, family vacations or determined spouses. In one way or another, we all managed to get caught in the web of Maine. What we have in common is a deep affection for this place.

We don't need brochures to tell us that Maine is full of natural beauty, interesting people, great communities, and a uniquely creative and wholesome energy. But for many Mainers, this isn't an easy place to live. A great environment and special character don't necessarily put good food in the refrigerator, give the kids a new pair of sneakers, keep the car running or the house warm in the winter.

We do all we can to preserve the beauty of this state, but Mainers also need an economy that allows us to live without worry and makes it possible for our children to stay here and raise their own families in Maine.

Part of our problem is that too many people in Maine feel that the economy is someone else's concern. Someone else will create the jobs or build the businesses or improve the laws. But it doesn't work that way. The health and vitality of Maine's economy has to be everyone's concern. Without a healthy economy, opportunities and hopes fade and frustrations and divisions grow. It becomes harder to raise the next generation of educated and engaged citizens, reduce poverty or protect the environment and character of Maine. At some point, it takes us to a downward spiral that is hard to escape.

Fixing our economy in Maine is the key to achieving nearly all of our shared dreams - and many of our personal ones.

WE'VE HAD OUR UPS AND DOWNS

Life in Maine was never easy, which is exactly why people here have had to be hard-working, tenacious, and resourceful. But it will surprise many Mainers to know we haven't always struggled with a weak economy. As you'll see in the next chapter, Maine has had more than its share of hard times, but also periods of prosperity and plenty.

By the late 19th century, in fact, Maine had become remarkably prosperous, thanks in part to the state's vast and rich natural resources. But it wasn't only because of good fortune that we became prosperous. It was also because we built a reputation for quality, trustworthiness and good value, first in shipbuilding and later in other products.

If you can hardly imagine Maine as a once-prosperous place, look around you and trust your eyes. Walk the neighborhoods of virtually any town in Maine with open access to the sea. You'll see sturdy and sometimes magnificent public buildings, homes, schools, and inspiring places of worship. You'll see public parks and libraries and museums. Elsewhere in the state, you'll find millions of acres of protected lands and state parks.

These are legacies meant to survive for centuries, rather than decades. They were handed down to us by the Mainers who came before our time, and those people have something important to teach us. Most of them faced far greater challenges than we'll ever know. They crossed dangerous oceans. Cleared land. Built houses and farms and communities. In time, they created small businesses to serve their local area, and in many case to serve the world.

They were frugal but not afraid to invest in the future. By combining imagination with pride in their work, they constantly improved old products and invented new ones. What they eventually created was not just buildings and communities, but also a resilient and vibrant economy. It was an economy that was not dependent upon a handful of large businesses that could fly away with a change of wind. Instead, it was built of thousands of small businesses with deep enough roots in their communities to weather the storms of change that so regularly blew across the state.

A TIME OF TRANSITION

For 50 years or more, Maine has been changing in some deeply unsettling ways, and we've barely understood it.

For most of Maine's history, we've relied on raw materials, farming, and manufacturing to sustain ourselves. Those jobs were all very labor intensive, which meant that they could support large families, bustling communities, and a culture of independence, hard work, and self-sufficiency, in all corners of the state.

In recent decades, many of those traditional Maine jobs have declined or even vanished altogether. They succumbed in some cases to competition from away but far more regularly to rapid mechanization that has eliminated tens of thousands of jobs.

Rural Maine and small towns away from the coast have been especially hard hit. Small farmers found themselves competing with industrial-scale, fully mechanized farming elsewhere. People who worked in the woods saw their jobs replaced by massive cutting machines. Thousands of small fishing boats up and down the coast disappeared as larger trawlers drove fish stocks further out to sea.

Similar technological changes have happened in our paper mills, driven by both changing consumer habits and technology. We're reading fewer things on paper and more on screens, which is reducing the demand for paper. The technology that is used to produce paper has also been changing, allowing us to manufacture nearly as much paper as we ever have, but with far fewer workers.

As more of our farms and mills have closed or shrunk, it's become much harder to stay put or find decent jobs, especially for people in rural Maine without technical or professional training and degrees.

In what seemed like the blink of an eye, farmers became commuters to make ends meet. Other people in rural Maine found jobs in the state's cities or remaining industries. Today, the remaining population of rural Maine is both smaller and older than it was once was. Communities and schools are struggling to stay afloat and to find volunteers and people to run for local office.

Those forces of change – competition and increasing mechanization – have left large swaths of Maine with more people than jobs. And that has produced a slow and reluctant trickle of migration from rural counties to southern and coastal ones and, in too many cases, it has continued further south and out of state, as Mainers have searched for jobs and opportunity.

This is a profound change in Maine's character, in what history will call a very short period of time. Rural Maine was once the bedrock of both the state's economy and its way of life. It was home to the bulk of our population, supporting generations of families and hundreds of communities.

All of this has lead us to confront some unwelcome realities. First among them is this: when jobs decline because of new technologies it's nearly impossible to bring them back. Not that we won't continue to have some good jobs in farming, forestry, and fishing, but we won't have anything like the labor-intensive jobs of the past that could support large populations in rural parts of the state.

There are, of course, some places where labor-intensive economies can be preserved – Maine's lobster industry, which limits the size of boats and crews, and the number of traps, is the closest example – but in most cases we aren't going to return to hand saws in the woods, families farming with horses, or hundreds of people running paper machines.

The good news for rural Maine is that there are encouraging signs in the new wave of local foods and organic growing. Young farmers are coming into Maine and learning to make farms work. Older farmers are working with nonprofit organizations to save their land and extend farming to the next generation.

We're also finding new uses for Maine's forests to produce everything from home-grown energy, with wood pellets, to biomass and furniture. And, we've begun to expand tourism into regions of Maine that are away from the coast.

All of that is helping Maine to become a more self-sufficient food and energy producer and exporter. And that is beginning to brighten the prospects for rural Maine. Agriculture, in particular, is now one of Maine's fastest-growing economic sectors, and it's getting younger.

The renewal in rural Maine, though it is still small, is being driven by exactly the kind of innovation and fresh thinking that the rest of the economy now needs. It embraces innovation, encourages smaller-scale and more sustainable practices and responds to changes in the marketplace that are demanding quality, character and healthy products – all the things that Maine is famous for.

GOING BACKWARDS IS NOT AN OPTION

Anyone who has lived in Maine for more than a few years, and particularly if they've lived in central, northern or Down East Maine, understands that whatever the statistics show or the politicians say, large parts of Maine have been in a recession for decades.

In my central Maine family, hard-working people with little education, but with a strong determination to succeed, were able to improve their lives because of good jobs in the mills or in the businesses that those mills supported.

They were able to buy homes, build camps, get better cars, and enjoy a good life. It was easy for them to believe in an even brighter future for their children.

In those days, people could walk out of high school and go to work in the mills or the woods or on a boat and be assured of a good living. And a college degree, for those able to attend college, was a virtual guarantee of a secure job and a good life without mountains of debt.

Then it began to erode before their eyes, as changes swept through Maine like a cold February wind.

The brief period of time when large numbers of working-class people could climb their way into a more comfortable middle class with lower-skill, high-wage jobs is all but over. Even while manufacturing is making a small comeback in America, it isn't expanding the middle class with it. In the most recent reports by the U.S. Department of Labor, more than 80 percent of the jobs where wages are projected to fall are in manufacturing.

All of this has left the children and grandchildren of the people who held those lost jobs wondering what would come next. Discouragement and pessimism set in, as faith in the future declined.

In the search for answers, Mainers have spent a long time trying to prop up the old economy and bring back yesterday's jobs. We've looked to our southern horizon in the futile hope that some major corporation would come and save us, just as a wave of mills did when they came here over a hundred years ago.

In the hardest-hit regions of Maine, we've increasingly looked to government to create more jobs in public schools or local offices, in road construction or with local college campuses. We've also tried to soften the blow of a declining economy and shrinking payrolls by expanding public assistance programs, which now help more than one in four Mainers.

Those actions have allowed us to tread water, barely, but done little to grow the next economy. It turns out that waiting for the clocks to run backward, or for someone to save us, is not much of a winning strategy for a new prosperity. In our case, it's been a dismal failure.

Today, we're seeing the full consequences of a lagging economy. Greater frustration and anger among voters. Deeper political and social divisions. Growing dependency not only on government programs but also on government jobs. Drug abuse and crime have appeared where little of either once existed.

Politics hasn't helped. Ever since our economic decline began, too many politicians have promised to bring back or hold on to old jobs, which none of them had the power to do. Politicians can promise many things, and deliver some of them, but turning back the tide of technology and history is not among them.

And it hasn't stopped. A few years back, a leading candidate for statewide office argued that the heart of Maine's future economy would be in forestry, fishing, and farming. It was a speech that ignored both technology and history, and was far better suited to an election in 1920 than one today.

But it was what some people desperately wanted to hear. Unfortunately, it only perpetuated the idea that if we just wait a little longer, or elect the right person, happy days will be here again.

GETTING BEYOND THE POISON OF PESSIMISM

Some Mainers seem defeated by the setbacks of the last few generations. They say that prosperity can't return to Maine. "We're too cold or remote. Taxes and energy costs are too high. The schools are no good. The government is corrupt." Those folks seem to believe that Maine can only fail. And by expressing those views, they're helping, in some ways, to fulfill those low expectations.

Maine has enormous potential to grow a new prosperity, but to achieve that potential, we'll first need to remove a few barriers that are blocking our way.

The first is an advanced infection of a crippling pessimism that has reached epidemic proportions in parts of Maine, over the last 30 to 40 years, and even now in parts of government. It's taken us on a downward spiral to nowhere, deepening our divisions and eroding our ability to work together.

Pessimism has a way of becoming self-fulfilling, as people lose hope in the future and stop doing the things that success requires. Once that disease takes hold in any society or organization, strong medicine must be applied before anything positive can happen.

This pessimism is now being encouraged by too many of our political leaders. Every campaign seems to bring more tearing down than building up, giving us more reasons to be cynical and angry than to be energized and hopeful. Over time, our spirit of hope and community is being poisoned in slow drops that ooze out of our televisions during every campaign season.

We're also seeing more people looking for someone to blame for a weak economy, whether it's political opponents, people on welfare, or immigrants fleeing worse conditions in their countries, as though anyone is to blame for a changing world economy and rapidly advancing technology.

These things have produced a new bad habit among our leaders. We are sending more and more downbeat and destructive messages about Maine to the world that are enormously harmful to our economy and that undermine what we are able to do in the future.

"It's impossible to grow a business here," say too many leaders in Maine. "Maine workers are either unskilled or lazy." "Regulations are onerous." "The state is overrun with welfare cheats."

If you owned a business in another state and were looking to relocate to a safe and beautiful place to grow your company and raise a family, why in the world would you want to be in a state whose leaders speak about it in that way? They're telling you to stay away.

Think about how messages like this work.

Imagine if you were visiting another state, walking in a community's downtown, and looking for a good place for dinner. You're standing outside a promising restaurant, perusing the menu in the front window. The entrees look great, but as you work down the list to the bottom of the page, you come to this.

THE FOOD IS SO-SO, THE STAFF CAN BE RUDE, AND WE'VE HAD A FEW RECENT CASES OF FOOD POISONING.

PLEASE SEAT YOURSELF.

It's not hard to imagine what you and any other sensible person would do – which would be to run to another restaurant.

That's pretty much what we've been saying about Maine to the rest of the world in recent years, and it shouldn't surprise us that while the country has been coming out of a long and deep recession, we're lagging behind almost every other state.

When people or places experience a long string of disappointments, they usually respond in one of two ways. Some become consumed with frustration or fear or anger, lamenting their misfortune, bad luck and circumstances. In short order, that response leads to angry scapegoating and circular firing squads.

Successful people, on the other hand, embrace another approach. They learn as much as possible from what they've been through, make a realistic assessment of the challenges and options they face, develop strategies to reach their goals, and get themselves going.

Look at every successful person or company or economy and what you will see is optimistic, resourceful, determined people. They try things. Sometimes they fail, but they always go right back at it. Over time, they usually find a way to succeed, and to bring others along with them.

The people who are building a new prosperity in Maine aren't mad as hell or discouraged. They're too busy doing things. They believe in the power of positive action, hard work, and personal responsibility. And they see Maine's glass as more than half full of great potential.

SOME ENCOURAGING NEWS

There are some encouraging developments in Maine today, and even more on the horizon. As you'll see in the chapters that follow, Maine is experiencing an upsurge of small startups and new smaller businesses, particularly in food, technology, and energy, but spreading now to other sectors.

Many of those businesses are finding inventive ways to blend old traditions with new ideas, produce new products, and grow companies from Kittery to Eastport. Innovation is becoming the economic engine of Maine. It's an engine with many moving parts, including new forms of microbusinesses, partnerships, and employee-owned ventures, fast-growing startups, and larger firms that have been busy reinventing themselves.

Maine's next economy isn't being imported or copied from California or Boston or North Carolina, though we can learn from all of them. It is emerging as something uniquely suited to Maine and reflecting who we are, what we care about, and how we operate.

The people who are building this next economy know what we have to do to succeed. We have to work as hard as we can, innovate in everything from businesses to schools to government, and produce quality products that strengthen our brand, and bring more resources to Maine.

By doing those things, we hope to make Maine a place that celebrates entrepreneurs and innovators who are creating new ideas and products that are distinctively from Maine.

One of the first steps in getting there is to better understand our past, and what it has to teach us.

REDISCOVERING OUR INNOVATIVE SPIRIT

THE RISE AND FALL OF MAINE'S ECONOMY

Colin Woodard, author and journalist

A century ago, a 40-year-old dry goods clerk with an eighth-grade education started stitching together a new kind of boot in a basement workshop from materials paid for with a $400 loan from his brother. The clerk, born and raised in Greenwood, Maine, was

an avid hunter and had hit upon what he thought would be ideal footwear for his backwoods outings: a waterproof rubber shoe stitched to comfortable, ankle-high leather uppers. He also had an inspired idea of how to find and entice potential customers: buy a mailing list of all persons who had applied for a state hunting license and offer the boot with a money-back guarantee, no questions asked.

The first shipment was a failure. The rubber lacked the appropriate qualities and tore away from the stitches, resulting in 90 percent of the clerk's orders being returned. Undaunted, the tinkerer—Leon Leonwood Bean—refunded every customer, borrowed another $400 from his brother, and collaborated with Boston's U.S. Rubber Company to perfect the design. The new boots were a hit, and remain so today, the hallmark of the company L. L. Bean built, which now has annual revenues of $1.5 billion, stores from Freeport to Tokyo, and 5,000 Maine-based employees.

Many others followed in L. L. Bean's footsteps to create new products that were met with stunning success around the globe. Tom and Kate Chappell built a personal care business called Tom's of Maine that started with an idea for an environmentally friendly laundry detergent and a $5,000 loan from a friend. Single mother Roxanne Quimby made a lip balm out of beekeeper Burt Shavitz's unused beeswax and created Burt's Bees. Jonathan King and Jim Stott sold homemade jam at the farmers' market and built Stonewall Kitchen. A family of modest hoteliers, the Rickers, began selling water from their Poland spring in 1859, founding a spa resort that hosted presidents and a bottling company now known around the world.

We're accustomed to thinking of our state as a backwater, its economy stunted because much of its territory lies too far from the life-giving sun of Boston and the East Coast megalopolis beyond. Our traditional industries—forest products, farming, and fishing—are a shadow of what they once were, while the forests, fields, and waterfront fill up with the second homes of people with the good sense to live in more hospitable economic climes. We see people come here to escape the hectic life of more prosperous places while so many of our friends, children, and grandchildren seek to escape our state in search of prosperity. It's made us a pessimistic lot, skeptical that we could ever build a thriving economy without ruining the sense of place that supports so  much of the economic activity we do have. If better days are to come, we think to ourselves, it will be by attracting factories and office parks from away, not by coaxing anything new from our state's thin, glacier-scraped soil.

We've forgotten that it wasn't always this way. A century and a half ago, Maine was a major player in the national economy, with a rapidly growing population and consummate influence over national politics. On the eve of the Civil War, our population was increasing by 8 percent a decade and was one of the youngest—not the oldest—in the Union. We had six seats in the U.S. Congress, more than California, Texas, and Florida combined. Our state was a storehouse of granite, ice, lumber, salt cod, lime, and foodstuffs—resources critical to the development of the rapidly expanding cities of the Atlantic and Gulf coasts.

We weren't a backwater at all—quite the opposite. Throughout the colonial period, Maine's island and peninsular communities had stood astride the major sea lanes connecting New and Old England. After independence, Maine farmers, fishermen, lumberjacks, and factory workers were plugged into the national economy by Maine's enormous merchant fleet, which dominated the coastal carrying trade, providing tens of thousands of jobs for sailors, shipbuilders, and dock workers in Portland, Bath, and beyond. Ships built, owned, and crewed by Mainers returned home from Southern ports with molasses for Portland's cavernous rum distillery and cotton for the rapidly expanding textile mills, which by 1860 accounted for almost a quarter of the state's economic output.

At the same time we had emerged as the largest lumber producer in the world, with Bangor the biggest lumber port on the entire planet. Our lumberjacks perfected techniques and technologies for moving enormous spruce and pine out of the forest and onto world markets, and later carried these to the Upper Great Lakes states and the Pacific Northwest, founding towns named Orono, Augusta, and Bangor in distant Wisconsin, Minnesota, and Washington State.

Mainers dominated the fishing industry, too, owning more than half the nation's offshore fishing vessels, and catching more cod, smoking more herring, and employing more full-time fishermen than any other state. Fortunes were made and invested in the tracts of genteel mansions that line now modest towns from Bath to Searsport, Fryeburg to Bangor, and Calais to Kingfield. "Our state has been blessed with the enjoyment of more than common health [and] the honest industry of the people in their various employments has been rewarded with success," Governor Albion Parris told the Legislature in 1823, as the boom was just beginning. "Our fisheries have been unusually prosperous; our farms have produced their common abundance, and our citizens exhibit generally the appearance of contentment and prosperity."

And then it all came crashing to the ground. The Civil War severed our ties with Southern markets, leaving most textile mills without cotton, rum distilleries without sugar, cod fishermen and ice cutters without access to much of their customer base. Confederate raiders harassed coastal shipping, which ground to a halt, leaving farmers with no way to get their produce to market in Boston and New York.

Fishing concerns collapsed as the cost of just about everything — marine insurance, salt, canvas, anchors, chains—increased geometrically. Shipyards in Bath went from building an average of 23 ships a year in the 1850s to just nine in 1861; the subsequent clash of the ironclads Monitor and Merrimac put an end to the era of wooden sailing vessels and, with them, most of state's shipbuilders and merchant fleets. Nor did things improve in peacetime, as the nation's commerce shifted from coastal sailing vessels to railroad networks, which were slow to develop in sparsely populated Maine.

Many Mainers who'd gone away to fight the war didn't come back, settling in the more fertile lands they'd encountered in the mid-Atlantic states and Ohio valley. As the economic catastrophe unfolded, others followed them in droves. Between 1860 and 1870, Maine actually lost population. Farms were abandoned to the elements. Ships rotted at anchor.

It's often said that Mainers are hardworking, self-reliant, and self-directed, and there's truth in that. But our people were forced to become so by dire circumstance: there were few jobs to be had, and those tended to be temporary. Survival in rural Maine—and that was most of Maine—required flexibility and tenacious resolve. Catch alewives, pick berries, cut wood, dig clams, and trap beavers, otter, lobsters, or herring, feed the tourists, repair tools or boats or plows, mow the summer people's lawns, take surplus vegetables and milk to market, help the neighbors press cider—many families pieced together a livelihood by seizing on seasonal opportunities, often teaching themselves how to make, fix, or produce a wide variety of things.

We became a state of tinkerers and inventors, less connected to the world but perhaps more connected to each other. Innovation became encoded into our cultural DNA.

That's not to say we didn't have large-scale employers. Indeed, the late 19th century saw an explosion of certain kinds of manufacturing, but they tended to be controlled from distant boardrooms and served supply chains outside rather than within Maine. The lumber industry had cut itself out of competitiveness, but once a method of making paper from wood pulp was perfected in the 1870s and 1880s, paper companies bought up their vast land holdings and built mills along the rivers. Textile mills, fish-packing plants, lobster canneries, and potato farms provided large numbers of low-wage jobs, often seasonal in nature and located in rural areas.

In the wake of the Second World War, a new downward spiral began, as globalization and technology conspired to change Maine's fortunes again. Many of these jobs vanished or were shipped to the southern United States, Mexico, Brazil, or China, where labor or inputs were even cheaper. We still have logging crews, but instead of a 12-person team armed with chainsaws and skidders, there are three-person teams with mechanized harvesters. The number of workers required to produce a given amount of paper fell by more than half between the mid-1970s and the mid-1990s. Our last sardine plant closed in 2011, and even L. L. Bean makes its products in Asia these days. As a result, manufacturing's share in statewide employment fell from 24 percent to 10 percent between 1980 and 2004. "No longer do the state's storied natural resources and manufacturing sectors anchor the economy," the Brookings Institution correctly noted in 2006, "and neither will they bounce back to previous levels."

Ironically, our 19th-century collapse encouraged the creation of another signature industry: tourism. The absence of industry, and sparse population, made the coast and interior lakes attractive to summer visitors escaping the crowded, polluted cities of that era. Wealthy summer people—Vanderbilts, Astors, and Rockefellers among them—built sprawling mansions and took steps to ensure their idyllic retreats were not sullied by factories, motor cars, or even bridges and highways.

We became Vacationland and, later, The Way Life Should Be, precisely because industry and settlement had failed to sully our landscapes, lakes, forests, and harbors. By accident, we had found ourselves with perhaps the greatest tracts of unspoiled space in the entire northeastern United States, much of it still replete with natural resources.

The Maine "brand"—first created by railroads to boost passenger traffic, perfected by resort hotels, L. L. Bean, and Down East magazine, and sustained by the Maine lobster—was built, tinkerer-like and haphazardly, on the ruins of our antebellum boom. Out of tragedy, we've inherited an increasingly scarce and valuable resource: a largely unspoiled natural and human environment.

Their example is now being replicated by hundreds and possibly thousands of others across the state, as they build a new economy driven by innovation and entrepreneurs.

 **Colin Woodard** is a *New York Times* bestselling author and award-winning journalist, where he writes about state and national affairs at the *Portland Press Herald* and *Maine Sunday Telegram*, where he won a George Polk Award for his investigative reporting and was named 2014 Journalist of the Year by the Maine Press Association. A Maine native and longtime foreign correspondent for *The Christian Science Monitor*, *The Chronicle of Higher Education* and *The San Francisco Chronicle*, he has reported from more than fifty countries.

He has written several popular books: American Nations: A History of The Eleven Rival Regional Cultures of North America (Viking Press, 2011), The Republic of Pirates: Being The True and Surprising Story of the Caribbean Pirates and the Man Who Brought Them Down (Harcourt, 2007), The Lobster Coast: Rebels, Rusticators, and the Struggle for a Forgotten Frontier (Viking Press, 2004), and Ocean's End: Travels Through Endangered Seas (Basic Books, 2000). His fifth book, American Character: A History of the Epic Struggle Between Individual Liberty and the Common Good, is scheduled for release in March 2016. His email is colin@colinwoodard.com.

MAINE HAS ALWAYS BEEN A STATE OF INNOVATORS

Steve Bromage, Maine Historical Society

Across the state, across sectors, people are talking about where Maine is headed.

People recognize that Maine faces real challenges: a struggling economy, an aging population, and not enough opportunities for young people who want to build lives and families here. Nonetheless, there is indeed a sense of opportunity: in the remarkable quality of life we enjoy; in the innovative, entrepreneurial spirit of Maine people; and in Maine's unique and very special sense of place.

The question we all grapple with is: How do we build a vibrant, sustainable future for Maine? A future that draws on and strengthens Maine's powerful sense of place, and imagines and shapes what a healthy Maine might look like 10, 20, 50 or 100 years from now.

Maine Historical Society

One of the most important things that history shows us is that change is dynamic and perpetual. Maine has evolved constantly for hundreds of years. There has not been a moment in time—1100, 1630, 1785, 1820, 1840, 1865, or 1970—when Maine was not dealing with changing markets, technology, populations, culture, natural environments, opportunities, and challenges.

By considering, embracing, and making use of that history, that *experience*, we can better understand the transitions that Maine is going through now, and be proactive in planning for and shaping Maine's future.

It's useful to consider how innovation and innovators have shaped Maine during earlier transitions. In each of the cases below—and in many, many others—Mainers recognized opportunity in the structure and nature of their contemporary economy. They understood markets, technology, and Maine's particular assets. They had foresight, made investments, took calculated risks, and became catalysts for a business, industry, community and/or region, and hence the state.

THE WABANAKI:
EARLY AND ONGOING INNOVATORS

The first people of Maine, the Wabanaki, were also Maine's earliest innovators. Creating and following traditional pathways, they moved seasonally to pursue opportunity, travelling to where resources, markets, and trading partners were. Sophisticated innovations, like ceramics and the development of the birch bark canoe, transformed regional trading networks, economies, and the structure of life. Later, by the mid-late 19th century, Wabanaki artists like Mary Pelagie Nicola (1775–1867), aka Molly Molasses, created an industry and sustained themselves in times of crisis by marketing traditional assets—baskets and other innovative art forms—to the emerging tourist market in Portland and other parts of the state. More recently, the Maine Indian Basketmakers Alliance, founded in 1993, became a pioneer in Maine's modern creative economy by re-establishing summer markets and mentoring artists in marketing.

JOHN WINTER AND EARLY TRADE

Maine's first Eurocentric economy was based on trade. The earliest semi-permanent European settlements in Maine were highly-competitive outposts set up to support the trade of fish and furs. Next time you are sitting on Crescent Beach in Cape Elizabeth, look across to Richmond Island, and imagine the activity that bustled there in the 1630s. John Winter ran a thriving operation there for his father-in-law, Robert Trelawny.

Trelawny and other English entrepreneurs, like John Popham and Sir Fernando Gorges, took advantage of Maine's location, its rich fishery, and other resources to build their personal wealth. This speaks to two critical facets of Maine's economic history: geography and sources of capital. One of Maine's first competitive advantages was its proximity to European markets (relative to the other colonies)—it was at the center of the Atlantic world. These trading posts also established a pattern: innovation and investment often came from away, extracted resources and value, and left when markets shifted.

SHEPHARD CARY:
BUILDING AN AROOSTOOK TIMBER EMPIRE

The extraction of natural resources has clearly defined Maine's economic history. But the industries, communities, and economic activity that grew out of those resources didn't materialize on their own. Enterprising businesspeople saw opportunity, invested, and capitalized. Consider Shepard Cary (1805–1866), an entrepreneur and important early leader in Aroostook County. He developed a tremendous operation in the County that built and supplied the U.S. Army base there, negotiated and managed trade on northern Maine rivers, and created a vast timber operation that, by the early 1840s, employed more than 2,000 people.

JOHN ALFRED POOR: FROM CANADIAN GRAIN TO THE PORTLAND COMPANY

In terms of foresight and hustle, there might be no more dramatic story than that of John Alfred Poor (1808–1871). In 1845, concerned about the state's economy, Poor saw a once-in-a-lifetime opportunity for Maine: Canada needed an ice-free winter port through which it could ship grain from the Canadian heartland to Europe. Facing direct competition from Boston, Poor undertook an epic sleigh ride from Montreal to Portland during a February blizzard to demonstrate that Portland provided a faster, more direct, and hence more economical route. He succeeded. Portland was selected, and a group of business leaders created the Atlantic and St. Lawrence Railroad with a loan from the city of Portland.

That, in turn, provided the catalyst for the founding of the Portland Company, whose steam engines, locomotives, pulp machines, and other industrial products were a major driver of economic activity in the state for more than a century. These interrelated industries attracted workers to Maine from around the world, drove the growth and vitality of Portland, and created the wealth that supported the founding of many of Maine's cultural and civic organizations.

Maine Historical Society

HUGH CHISOLM AND THE CREATION
OF MAINE'S PAPER INDUSTRY

After the Civil War and as the nation's center of gravity moved west, the market for Maine timber shifted—it wasn't efficient to get Maine lumber to the most quickly-growing markets. At the same time, the country's growing population, cities, economy, and literacy created an incredible demand for paper—for publishing, packaging, and countless other uses. Entrepreneurs like Hugh Chisolm (1847–1912) recognized that the state had the elements needed to turn Maine into the nation's primary supplier of paper. Instead of masts or lumber, Maine's trees would be used to produce pulp. Chisolm carefully surveyed the state's geography, identified Pennacook Falls in Rumford as an unparalleled source of power, built state-of-the-art paper mills there (and in other places), connected Rumford to the national rail line, and helped establish the paper industry as a dominant force in Maine's economy, culture, and identity.

NATHAN AND ISAAC WINSLOW:
CANNING MAINE'S WAY TO PROSPERITY

Today, Maine is particularly proud of its foodie culture, an important piece of the state's contemporary economy and identity. Contemporary foodways—growing, selling, buying and eating locally—are in fact traditional foodways, and reflect the way that Mainers have eaten for most of the state's history. The current farming renaissance in Maine returns us to important parts of our agricultural heritage. The example of innovation I want to share, though, seems to run counter to our contemporary craving for freshness: canning. One of the ways Maine compensated for its distance from markets was by developing alternative ways to process, store, and transport foods.

In the 1850s, Nathan Winslow (1785–1861) and Isaac Winslow (1787–1869), both of Portland, were among the first in the United States to develop a viable canning process—which, in turn, led to the development of one of Maine's most important 19th–20th century industries. Maine's extensive farming infrastructure, well-developed seaports, and proximity to East Coast cities made the state an ideal place for canning operations. Canning factories were usually built within farming communities. By the early 1900s, Maine had 111 vegetable canneries, and every autumn, the canning industry employed thousands of Maine men, women, and children.

A CASE STUDY IN INFRASTRUCTURE:
CENTRAL MAINE POWER COMPANY

At the same time Maine innovators built businesses, industries, and communities, they also recognized the need to invest in infrastructure: Chisolm's success was contingent on connecting Maine's paper mills to national rail lines; the canning industry drew on an abundance of farms and produce. Consider the electrification of Maine: After the first electric light in Maine was lit at the Willimantic wood products mill at Greeley's Falls in Piscataquis County in 1880, intrigued first-adaptors—a combination of tinkerers, investors, business people, and local leaders—saw magic and potential.

Maine's streams and rivers had powered mills for processing grain and milling lumber since early settlement and, by the mid-19th century, modern industry. Then, visionaries saw, the state's streams and rivers could generate electricity. Initially the technology was crude—the electricity generated was weak, couldn't be stored, and could only be transmitted short distances. But the technology evolved, and soon electricity could be captured efficiently, transmitted farther, and used for a broad range of industrial, commercial, and domestic functions.

In 1899, Walter Wyman (1874–1942) and his partner Harvey Eaton purchased the Oakland Electric Light Company, improved its infrastructure, and then began purchasing and pulling together small, community-based power companies. By 1910, Central Maine Power Co. had been formed.

At first, people couldn't imagine why they would want or need electricity, or what they would use it for. CMP created retail stores to sell electric appliances—they sold electric stoves made to look like traditional woodstoves to get people comfortable with the idea and to begin to build a domestic market for electricity. By the 1910s, photographs show how the arrival of electricity was transforming Maine's landscape and communities, and "modernizing" the state. Linemen developed and improved the electrical infrastructure on the ground as they installed and maintained it, and their innovations were essential.

By the 1920s, the Maine legislature fought fierce battles about the development and principles of the grid: Who had rights to Maine-generated electricity? Could it be transmitted out of state? Who should profit? These were contentious and highly charged issues. More broadly, Mainers didn't know precisely how electricity might change Maine and its economy, but it was clear that electricity was the future. The parallels to contemporary discussions about broadband infrastructure are uncanny. We can't imagine all of the ways that it will change our lives or define every opportunity it will create, but there is no doubt that broadband will be essential to Maine's next economy.

What do these stories tell us? That businesses, industries, economies, and healthy communities don't spring up spontaneously. It takes foresight, vision, collaboration, shrewd practicality, and investment to build a vibrant Maine. There are countless other examples. Maine history provides an invaluable body of experience to draw on as we look at the world today and identify Maine's best opportunities—and then seize them.

 **Steve Bromage** is Executive Director of the Maine Historical Society where he has worked since 2001. Founded in 1822, MHS promotes the preservation and dynamic use of Maine history and provides outreach, training, and educational services throughout the state. Among other initiatives, Steve has helped guide the development of the Maine Memory Network (www.mainememory.net), a nationally-recognized statewide digital museum that features online contributions from more than 270 organizations across Maine. Previously, Steve helped found the online *Disability History Museum* (http://www.disabilitymuseum.org/) and produce the award-winning NPR documentary *Beyond Affliction: The Disability History Project.*

THE BUILDING BLOCKS OF THE NEXT ECONOMY

For the next economy to grow more quickly, we're going to need more than just a good attitude and dedicated innovators. In the following chapters, some of Maine's best thinkers and doers share their ideas on what needs to happen to create both the culture and the infrastructure that will allow Maine to flourish.

INNOVATION AND ENTREPRENEURS ARE KEY

Catherine Renault, Innovation PolicyWorks

To grow a new prosperity in Maine we need to embrace the idea that creativity, innovation, and entrepreneurship are the driving forces of the next economy, and not just something that we tack on to a long list of things we're interested in. It requires that we get behind our innovators and entrepreneurs in a big way, to ensure that they have the tools they need to succeed.

Building that kind of economy requires us to create a culture that encourages and supports innovators and entrepreneurs, where we're not afraid to think big, take risks, stumble if necessary on the path forward, and seize our full potential. It also requires us to create an innovation ecosystem that makes starting, running, and growing businesses easier.

Here's a little-known secret about the economy: innovative companies grow faster, have higher profits, and pay higher wages. It doesn't matter whether they're big or small, high tech or no tech, in a city or in rural areas. Innovation can happen in new industries or older ones, in for-profits or not-for-profits and in multigenerational companies that are constantly reinventing themselves, or start-ups and scale-ups working in garages, small offices or new campuses.

After all, innovation simply means a new idea or way of doing things or a new product that somebody somewhere cares enough about to buy. Most Maine companies start with a new idea; the real trick is to keep innovating.

And, innovative companies end up in places that support the creativity it takes to constantly learn and grow, place where it's all right to say: I don't know. I need to learn more. I fail a lot. This is why innovative companies can often be found in the same places where there are lot of artists, writers, and other creative people.

The question now is: how can Maine accelerate that growth? How can we create more budding entrepreneurs and help more existing businesses and emerging success stories to innovate, and to believe in themselves enough to leap to the next level? And how can we create the communities where these companies and entrepreneurs will thrive?

We've struggled for years to find the right path to a new prosperity, looking in all directions and chasing one fad after another. Meanwhile, the foundations of tomorrow's economy are all around us, in our communities and in our new and existing companies.

There are two distinctly different paths forward for Maine's economy. One is to continue to chase the dream of attracting big companies to Maine that will provide thousands of jobs overnight. Think of that as the "hitting the lottery" approach, or a hunting expedition that's all about catching a wooly mammoth, where we dangle lots of tax breaks and goodies on the end of a line.

We've been looking for those big deals for decades, and it hasn't produced much of anything. Even if it had, it's an extremely expensive way to grow an economy—and one that leaves us vulnerable to the ups and downs of a few large employers. And to be competitive with the states in the South for which this is a way of life, we would have to invest millions of dollars more each year in this effort. The other way forward is to build tomorrow's economy from the ground up, on a firm foundation of our strengths and skills, our powerful brand, and our talent for invention.

That is an approach that appreciates the value of building the next economy one new job at a time, and has us investing in ourselves rather than in big tax breaks. It leads us to invest in better education, grants and loans to start and expand businesses, and research and development that can fuel both new and existing businesses that want to create new products and services, invent new business models, or streamline their operations.

It also suggest that we invest in our communities, in our historic buildings and downtowns, whose unique character provides an antidote to the cookie-cutter and antiseptic places that many entrepreneurs want to avoid. We should recognize that creativity and innovation can provide the focus and impetus to bring back the economies of our towns, big and small, by attracting young entrepreneurs and their energy, ideas, and talents.

Lastly, investing in innovation means that we have to embrace a more diverse and tolerant culture, because that's what it takes for creativity to flourish. Good ideas often come from the collisions of knowledge from difference disciplines, cultures, or perspectives. Diverse and tolerant places also attract creative people, who in turn attract the highly educated knowledge workers who will power Maine's next economy.

Some of that ecosystem is already in place, with organizations like the Finance Authority of Maine, the Maine Technology Institute, the Maine Center for Entrepreneurial Development, and promising initiatives in education. But to become a state that is really an incubator of new ideas and products, we're going to need to put that small infrastructure on steroids, and build a seamless "feeder system" that encourages budding entrepreneurs and startups to move toward becoming tomorrow's success stories.

It means building a network of communities—some call them "innovation hubs"—that support entrepreneurs where they are, while also linking them into a broader ecosystem in Maine and across the country. It means making sure there are places where entrepreneurs and innovators can gather and work together, to learn from one another and partner with each other and with more established companies. It means teaming together to share our knowledge and resources, rather than each starting from scratch.

We have an opportunity today to build a new economy in Maine, propelled by creativity, innovation, and entrepreneurship, and relying upon the resourcefulness of Maine people. We can rebuild and revitalize our communities in the same way, bringing back our young people and attracting newcomers, to enjoy a vibrant economy.

 **Catherine Renault** is the principal and owner of Innovation Policyworks LLC, whose research and analysis enables Maine economic development officials to make more data-driven decisions for program improvement and policymaking. Dr. Renault also heads the board of directors of the Maine Center for Entrepreneurial Development and the board of managers for Sea Change Group LLC. She holds a research appointment at the University of Maine with the Foster Center for Student Innovation. Her 24 years of experience in state technology-based economic development and evaluation includes the directorship of the Maine Office of Innovation and service as Governor John Baldacci's science advisor, and previous work as managing director of Virginia's Center for Innovative Technology. She also spent 10 years in the private sector, including AT&T and Data General. A Boston native, she holds a Ph.D. from the University of North Carolina at Chapel Hill.

A FEEDER SYSTEM FOR A NEW ECONOMY

Don Gooding, Maine Center for Entrepreneurial Development

A Maine economy that is growing from the bottom up will require lots of companies, lots of helpers, lots of qualified employees, lots of entrepreneurs and business owners who want to grow. But how many companies? What kind? Where will they come from? What do they need to succeed? These are important questions to answer if we want to move from bold ambitions to specific action plans.

First, it's useful to put Maine's situation in the national context. Across the United States, employment growth comes predominantly from a small number of so-called "gazelle" companies, named by economist David Birch in 1994. He estimated that at any given time, 4 percent of employer-based companies (that is, not counting the self-employed) generate around 70 percent of all net new jobs.

How many gazelles would we need in Maine? With about 35,000 employers in the state, 1,400 growing rapidly would do the trick. These are companies that are at least doubling in revenue every four years, according to Birch's categorization.

The good news is that they don't have to be any particular kind of business, or one that we can't support in Maine. The national data shows that the most rapidly growing companies in the United States can be found in quite diverse industries. You can check out the annual listing of the Inc. 5000, published by Inc. Magazine, to see that diversity. That's good news for Maine, since our fastest-growing companies today are also diverse.

It's also good news that our below-average rate of venture capital investment won't inhibit growth. Studies of the *Inc.* 500—the very top of the fast growers—show only about 15 percent raised venture capital before appearing on the list. Maine is not without companies capitalized this way—Putney, BlueTarp Financial, CashStar, and iVantage Health Analytics have more than $150 million of venture capital among them. But the *Inc.* 5000 is full of bootstrapped companies—those that mostly rely on their own financial resources—so the lack of copious amounts of venture capital needn't be a barrier to building a legion of high-growth Maine firms.

How many do we have now? Unfortunately, we don't have a good answer. It's a fair guess that we don't have nearly enough, and yet we have more than most people think. Part of Maine's culture is to hide success, to keep our rapidly growing companies literally hidden in the woods. In our work building Maine's community of high-aspiration companies, we continue to find new companies quietly executing big dreams. Our guess, no more than that, is we have 500 high-aspiration firms—those that want to hit *Inc.* 5000 growth rates—but fewer than 200 that are actually running like gazelles.

Where will the next generation of Maine's gazelles come from?

We think many will be young companies—the Kauffman Foundation has found that lots of job growth comes from companies in their first five years—but it's certainly possible for many existing businesses to become a gazelle.

Step one for any new or existing business to grow gazelle horns is to think that growth is possible and desirable. Part of the work to be done is to help Maine entrepreneurs think big (and then think bigger), and to take steps towards achieving these high ambitions, because not everyone running a business or starting a new one has high aspirations. In fact, most do what they do to generate a decent income, not generate lots of new jobs for Maine. Importantly, this attitude is *not* just confined to Maine. A University of Chicago study showed that about 90 percent of young companies across the United States fall into this category of "income entrepreneurs" (a term we prefer to the somewhat derogatory "lifestyle business").

The Maine Center for Entrepreneurial Development (MCED) works with about 150 high-ambition entrepreneurs a year, a number that has grown from 15 a year in 2010. Their ambition is a critical first step, but of course not all 150 will even survive the subsequent two years, let alone achieve their ambitious revenue goals. Those that make it into MCED's Top Gun program—more than 30 in 2015—do increase their odds of survival, which is 78 percent historically vs. a national average of 50 percent of start-ups surviving to year five.

It's important to remember this fact of entrepreneurial development—success of any individual effort is not guaranteed, so you need lots of people and companies and ideas at every stage of development (an "entrepreneurial portfolio") to eventually achieve that critical mass of rapidly growing companies. Some baby gazelles get eaten by lions. Our first guess, then, is we need at least 150 new high-ambition companies a year to head toward a big statewide gazelle herd.

We also think there's no reason every Maine County can't have its share of rapidly growing companies. There will just be fewer in Knox than in Cumberland, because Knox has fewer people. But if we want growth statewide, it's important that every county knows how many gazelles ought to be running alongside their moose.

What will these high-ambition people be doing just before they set off on their path towards a bigger future? Some will be research spin-offs from our universities and places like the Jackson Laboratory in Bar Harbor and the Bigelow Laboratory for Ocean

Sciences in East Boothbay. Some will be college students aspiring to win a business pitch competition who end up with an enduring business that launches in Maine.

Some will be large companies like Sappi Fine Paper, which invest heavily in research and development to reinvigorate an old business. Some will form during a start-up weekend, a 72-hour race that starts from an undeveloped idea on Friday night and finishes with a business launching by Sunday evening.

Others will be existing Maine businesses sold to and revived by people "retiring" to Maine; others will be family businesses re-energized when a new generation takes over.

Some will come from the 30-plus young companies now working with mentors and peers in the Top Gun program going on in Portland, Orono, and Rockland. Some will come from out of nowhere and succeed with no assistance from the numerous programs Maine offers.

All of these are needed and more.

We need the equivalent of a sales funnel of growing companies: lots and lots at the beginning of the process to make sure we get enough rapidly growing ones coming out the other end. Companies starting or re-starting the path towards rapid growth experience a roller-coaster along the way; it is anything but a linear or simple "hockey stick" process. And the national data show revenue and jobs growth isn't forever, so Maine (like everywhere else) needs a never-ending supply of newly ambitious growth pioneers every year.

# of employees per company	1-4	5-9	10-19	20-49	50-99	100-249	250-499	500-999	1,000+	Total
1,000 companies @ national average	500	273	94	64	43	15	8	2	1	1,000
Average number of employees	2.5	7.5	14	32	70	150	325	675	1,500	
Total employees	1,250	2,048	1,316	2,048	3,010	2,250	2,600	1,350	1,500	17,372
Average annual employee gains	12%	12%	12%	12%	12%	12%	12%	12%	12%	
Annual employee gains	150	246	158	246	361	270	312	162	180	2,085

The good news is that the Maine sales funnel of high-aspiration companies is growing rapidly right now. Since 2010 there has been a noticeable uptick at the beginning of the funnel, even if it isn't showing up yet in aggregate employment data. We'd guess there are perhaps 500 high-aspiration companies across the state—firms that would aspire to *Inc.* 5000 growth rates, which is a minimum of 40 percent growth over three years.

I'd like to suggest a common goal: Build a statewide community of 1,000 high-ambition companies generating 2,000 net new jobs every year by 2020.

As you can see from the chart above, if those 1,000 companies are distributed in terms of their employees the same as the national average, and they grow employees on average 12 percent at every size level, then they are generating 2,000 jobs a year.

The good news is that building this jobs engine doesn't require giant companies. Maine has a high concentration of very small businesses, but it's also true nationally that 50 percent of all employer-based businesses have only one to four employees. We need many hundreds of Maine's smallest businesses to help build the economy, not just the few with 500 or more employees.

To hit this target of 1,000 growth-oriented companies generating 2,000 new jobs a year by the bicentennial, we estimate that Maine needs about 150 new high-aspiration companies every year. Many will be start-ups, some will be existing businesses refreshing their outlook. Not all of the 150 will make it to the finish line, or even out of the starting gate. We need more to build this coalition of growth, but we also need those who are quietly succeeding to let people know that it's very much possible to run a successful growing business in Maine.

And then, we need everybody to help them grow. Not just business counseling, but new talent, mentors and board members, good legal and accounting and marketing advice, capital from many sources, willing early customers, connections to national and international distribution and supply chains, researchers to solve problems and develop appropriate technologies, developers and real estate owners to pave the way, state and local governments to act like growing businesses are welcome.

It takes a village to help companies grow. We have what it takes to get to the vision of gazelles leaping across Maine. We just need to accelerate the progress we're making.

Don Gooding is the Executive Director of the Maine Center for Entrepreneurial Development and host of the television show Greenlight Maine, which promotes new business development. He is a former vice chairman of the Maine Angels, a group of investors that supports early-stage companies. He also has lectured on innovation and entrepreneurship at several Maine colleges and universities. Previously he was a telecommunications market analyst and venture capitalist for sixteen years, founded and ran a global specialty music business for another sixteen years, and has been a Maine Angels investor since the late 1990s. As the research partner for ten years for Accel Partners, a California-based firm that funds fledgling companies, he evaluated new telecom and datacom investment opportunities. In 1992, he founded a music venture that grew to include the world's largest source of a cappella music, a student a cappella performance program, and a sheet music publishing company.

SMALL IS NOT ONLY BEAUTIFUL, IT'S ESSENTIAL
THE ROLE OF MICROBUSINESSES IN MAINE'S FUTURE

Eloise Vitelli, New Ventures Maine

They are everywhere. And there are a lot of them. Walk down any Main Street or drive along the back roads and byways in any county in this state, and you will find them: retail shops of all stripes, web designers, chocolatiers and cheese makers, artists and craftsmen, child care providers, barbers and beauty salons, contractors and builders, accountants and architects, farmers, landscapers, massage therapists, bed and breakfast hosts—the list goes on.

They are one, two and five-person shops that are home-grown and rooted in our communities. If we want to grow Maine's next economy from the ground up, we need to pay attention to the smallest of our enterprises.

Microbusinesses are, in many ways, the foundation of the next economy. There were 133,230 microenterprises, defined as a business with four or fewer employees, in Maine in 2012, and they provided 21.6 percent of all jobs. In some counties—Washington and Knox, for example—a third of all employment comes from microbusinesses. Maine is second only to Vermont among New England states in the size of our microbusiness sector and ahead of the national rate of 19.1 percent.

In a state known for its ingenuity, self-reliance, and work ethic, it should come as no surprise that we have a high rate of self-employment and small-business creation. Microenterprises are woven into the very fabric of our state's economy and though each is by definition small, they collectively make a significant contribution to our economy, our communities, and our workforce.

The Association for Enterprise Opportunity, the national trade association for the microenterprise industry, reports that 92 percent of all U.S. businesses are microenterprises, and pegs the number of jobs created by micro enterprises at 41.3 million.[1] Research on the economic impact of Maine's microenterprise economy finds that for every two jobs created by a microbusiness, an additional 1.5 jobs are created somewhere else in the economy. Furthermore, these enterprises are estimated to contribute 13.2 percent to the state gross product.[2]

Microbusinesses add value to the lives of Maine residents and contribute to the Maine brand, providing an array of goods and services in all sectors—retail, personal and business services, and our more traditional farming, fishing, and forestry—attracting visitors who come to enjoy Maine "the way life should be."

A gourmet chocolate shop in Lubec, for example, with up to eight employees in peak season, has helped lure visitors from as far away as Mexico and England to this tiny coastal town at the far end of our state. A sled-dog company based in Augusta adds to the attraction of Maine winter sports and connects Maine with outdoors enthusiasts from far away.

In every community, the local carpenters, electricians, plumbers, painters, and roofers have helped build, repair, and maintain our homes, camps, and workplaces. Self-employed landscapers, contractors, and cleaning services maintain gardens, lawns, and living spaces, and plow and repair roads and driveways. The owner of a midcoast property management company hires many of these

---

[1] Association for Enterprise Opportunity, 2014.
[2] (Dr. James C. McConnon, 2009, updated annually).

same small operators, believing that her success is based upon the strong working relationships she forges with other local businesses. Because her business involves vacation rentals, she brings tourism dollars into the state as well.

Similarly, the owner of a Portland boutique, like many other retail craft centers around the state, features fine crafts that are strictly "made in Maine," directly promoting the Maine brand while giving market access to other self-employed individuals. Located in Portland's Upper Arts District, this retailer also sources 95 percent of her operating supplies from vendors in the area —everything from a credit card processor to shopping bags and other printing needs, further adding value to the local economy.

"Buy local" campaigns keep dollars recirculating in the local economy; they support and are supported by our microbusinesses; downtown revitalization projects rely on the participation of small and larger businesses to create diverse, vibrant Main Streets.

Microbusinesses create jobs for local people, not least of all the owner, and creating opportunities for individuals who might otherwise be left behind: women, minorities, disabled individuals, and younger workers, as well as older laid-off workers. Self-employment has long been the road that immigrants to this country have taken to economic self-determination and prosperity, and it has provided a pathway out of poverty for many others willing to take risks and work hard.

As they grow or expand to take advantage of seasonal or market changes, these enterprises provide critical work experience and on-the-job skills training to local people, like the painter who regularly hires a team of 18-to-24-year-olds in the spring. Along with their wages, he gives these young workers the opportunity to learn good work habits, punctuality, and teamwork, as well as industry-specific skills.

Nationally, while most jobs are created by entities with 20 or fewer employees, representing about 90 percent of all businesses, better-quality jobs, as measured by higher wages, benefits, and longevity, are thought to be provided by larger corporations.[1] More recently, however, the lingering effects of the Great Recession, particularly wage stagnation, suggest that employment quality among small and microenterprises may be catching up.

While many microbusinesses stay small by design, others grow and contribute further to Maine's economy. Coffee by Design started 21 years ago with one coffee shop in a downtown section of Portland that had a 40 percent vacancy rate. Today it has 45 employees in four locations and is selling wholesale coffee around the country. Successful, enduring businesses—of any size—are those that are able to innovate, respond, and adapt to changes in markets, technology, and other environmental factors. Giving birth to a business idea and working day to day to keep it alive and growing takes creativity, vision, and problem solving—the key ingredients for innovation.

It's been estimated that by 2018, 24 million workers in this country will be part of the "independent" workforce, a group that includes consultants, contractors, and contingent workers as well as sole proprietors and microbusiness owners. Half of all workers will be self-employed at some point in their careers, suggesting that our microenterprise economy will play an ever-greater role in preparing the workforce of the future as more of us need to develop an innovative, creative, entrepreneurial spirit.

The microenterprise economy, where individuals learn to innovate, is akin to the salt marsh, the economic brine that supports a diversity of life forms; it serves as a spawning ground for new ideas, and provides necessary nutrients for other, larger entities.

---

[1] Kansas Federal Reserve

Biologists and ecologists remind us how vital the salt marsh is, how dependent we are on the health and productivity of these wetlands.

To grow our economy, we need to protect the salt marsh; we need to scale our resources so that microenterprises remain strong and

resilient and so that those with the desire and the potential will find their way out to sea and grow into bigger businesses.

 **Eloise Vitelli** is the program and policy director for New Ventures Maine, a statewide organization helping Maine people achieve economic success. In 1984, she designed New Ventures, an entrepreneurship training program that helps aspiring entrepreneurs write business plans. She helped to establish and provided management support to the Maine Enterprise Option program, a collaborative project helping unemployment insurance recipients start small businesses. She helped bring Family Development Accounts, a matched savings and asset development program for low-income people, to Maine. She served on the Maine Economic Growth Council, was a member and past president of the Mid-Coast Economic Development District, and headed the Permanent Commission on the Status of Women. She was inducted into the Maine Women's Hall of Fame in 1995, the same year she attended the International Women's Conference in Beijing, China. She was elected to the state Senate in a special election in 2013, and served one year.

GROWING WITHOUT WRECKING THE PLACE

George Smith, Outdoor enthusiast and author

Mainers have appreciated—and been protective of—our amazing woods and waters for decades. Tourists who visit us here and who drive our economy may come to eat lobster and see a lighthouse, but they also value and enjoy the spectacular beauty of this place.

Unfortunately, as the old saying goes, we can't eat the scenery. And that sometimes forces us to lose our focus on protecting what we love, jeopardizing those very places and resources that make Maine special. Do we maximize that forest harvest or protect deer yards? Is that mountaintop best left alone or used for wind towers? Can we enjoy our lawns, growing right down to the water, or must we rip them up to protect water quality?

Or can we have it all and still protect what makes this state special? I say we can protect critical wildlife habitat and still cut lots of trees, place wind towers in the right places without ruining our mountain tops, have beautiful lawns with protective buffers along the lakes, and even—in my dreams—become energy independent.

We know that Mainers support all of these initiatives. Their strong support for the Land for Maine's Future Program demonstrates this. Since it was created in 1987, LMF has helped conserve 550,000 acres of our best places, using an average of $4.78 million annually, for an average cost of just $113 an acre. And we also know that conservation pays. The Trust for Public Land found that every $1 invested in land conservation through LMF returned an astonishing $11 in natural goods and services to the Maine economy. And that return increases every year.

As a hunter, I am especially grateful for LMF's purchases. Our hunting opportunities have been greatly diminished by an epidemic of private land posting, making public lands of growing importance as we seek to protect our outdoor heritage.

As an avid angler, I'm also well aware that we have no rights of access to moving water—our beautiful brooks, streams, and rivers. If someone owns both sides of a brook, and posts that land, I can't even stand in the water and fish, nor can you anchor your canoe there. Many years ago I played a role in dedicating 10 percent of LMF's money to water access, and almost every LMF project includes frontage of some water body.

I am also thankful for the thousands of volunteers who work for local land trusts, fish and game clubs, snowmobile and ATV clubs, and lake associations, to enhance, protect, and care for our public lands, trails, and water access sites. Private landowners who allow us to recreate on their property, enjoying everything from hunting to hiking to fiddle-heading and birding, also deserve our thanks and appreciation. Many people don't realize that our outdoor economy depends on all of these people (and yes, we are getting older and are in need of younger volunteers).

I write and worry a lot about rural Maine. When Linda and I began writing our weekly travel column, the Travelin' Maine(rs), for the *Kennebec Journal* and *Morning Sentinel*, we intended to focus on inland places, but everyone wants to go to the coast, so we do write columns about places there. Various initiatives are underway, including the Maine Woods Consortium, to boost inland tourism, but it's a tough challenge.

The thousands of paper industry jobs we've lost are not coming back, although we still have a strong forest industry, including biomass plants, sawmills, and pellet mills. But we've lost resources from inland to the coast, including deer and moose, brook trout and haddock and cod, and we face needs all across the economy, from fast Internet service to rail and road and bridge improvements. I can only hope we won't all have to live in and around Portland to find work!

There are reasons to be hopeful about our future here, including the Maine Sustainable Fisheries Initiative, organized by the Gulf of Maine Research Institute and some of Maine's outstanding chefs, to encourage restaurants to use underutilized fish species like hake. Forget haddock. Eat hake!

And while it took us years to convince the Legislature to designate our native brook trout as our Heritage Fish and protect them in waters that have never been stocked, we are now focused on this unique resource. But this might turn out to be for naught, because climate change threatens the cold water temperatures that brook trout need.

Perhaps we should all ask ourselves the question that Roger Brooks posed a while back in Greenville: "What do we want to be known for?" A Greenville group has been working to answer that question with the help of Brooks, an internationally known community branding expert.

Roger noted that class sizes in the local school have declined from 57 pupils to just seven, during the years the people on the Branding Initiative Committee have lived in Greenville. And he didn't hesitate to point out the obvious: "You need to differentiate Moosehead Lake from the other 502 Maine communities—and others in New England. You need a year-round sustainable economy," he said. "Mills aren't coming back." And that's the harsh truth that has yet to be recognized in some rural Maine towns, especially Millinocket, just north of Greenville.

Roger also didn't hide the fact that Greenville could take another path. "There are more ghost towns in America than ever before," he said. Something to think about. A good motivator, for sure. For all of us. But as we struggle to build a sustainable economy and state, let's be careful not to wreck the place.

 **George Smith** writes an award-winning outdoor blog for his website, georgesmithmaine.com and the *Bangor Daily News* website, and columns for the *Kennebec Journal* and *Waterville Morning Sentinel* and *The Maine Sportsman* magazine. As executive director of the Sportsman's Alliance of Maine for 18 years, he made it one of the state's most influential organizations before leaving in 2010 to write full time. For many years he also co-hosted Wildfire, a television show about hunting, fishing, conservation, and environmental issues. A Mount Vernon resident, he served on the Winthrop Town Council, the Mount Vernon Board of Selectman, the Kennebec County Commission, and the Mount Vernon Planning Board, as well as several state government committees and task forces. Politically, he worked to successfully defend moose hunting in a 1983 referendum, managed a 1992 campaign placing the Maine Inland Fisheries & Wildlife Department in the state constitution and protecting its revenues, and led a 2004 campaign that blocked a referendum seeking to end Maine's bear hunt.

FARMING'S REVIVAL OFFERS LESSONS FOR THE REST OF THE ECONOMY

John Piotti, Maine Farmland Trust

After decades of decline, farming in Maine is growing and ready to blossom. Maine is poised to build a vibrant farm economy—and to be become the "food basket of New England."

The rebirth of farming in Maine is a compelling story, full of lessons that may hold promise for the rest of Maine's economy. And I'm pleased to share some of those lessons. But I'm also cautious. That's because part of what I've learned from working with farmers over the last 20-plus years is that farming in Maine defies easy characterization.

Nina Young of Maine Farmland Trust and dairy farmer Tom Drew at Maple Meadow Farm Fest, Mapleton, Maine. Photo by

Farming here is at once "robust, thriving, threatened, modern, ancient, venerable, dirty, tedious, and hip." It's as diverse and complex as the thousands of Mainers who farm. And the story is that much more complicated because the recent growth of Maine farming has been uneven.

These nuances make it more difficult to describe farming in Maine, but they in no way diminish the fact that something big is happening here. And what's happening here suggests a way we might rebuild our rural economy around a new crop of small businesses—businesses rooted in Maine's unique assets, and positioned around the world that is coming.

The first clear signs of the rebirth of farming in Maine appeared in the federal agricultural census of 2002. Then from 2002 to 2007, the number of farms in Maine increased by almost a thousand,

from 7,199 to 8,136. By 2012, the value of farm production was up 24 percent over 2007, showing that new operations were not all small hobby farms, as some had suspected.

Meanwhile, from 2007 to 2012, the number of farmers in Maine who have been operating farms for less than three years grew by 49 percent, from 250 to 373, while dropping 25 percent  nationally. So here in Maine, the state with the oldest population in America, and where we are so concerned about the loss of young talent, we are breaking records in attracting beginning farmers. What a promising story!

But not all is rosy. While many farms are thriving, many others are struggling, and many more remain in business only because the farmers are willing to work exceptionally hard for little money. So it's also a complex story.

One way to think about agriculture in Maine is to recognize that during the last 20 years, farming here has followed two different tracks. The first track—commodity agriculture—includes those farms that sell their products principally to processors or wholesalers. In Maine, that includes many, though not all, of our dairy farms, potato farms, and blueberry farms.

The second track includes farms that may be raising some of these same products, though most of them are raising mixed vegetables or small livestock. Most of Maine's smaller farms fall into this second track, though some larger farms do as well. And many of Maine's organic farms fall into this track, though so do more than a few conventional farms.

Simply put, what distinguishes a farm in the second track from one in the first is not a farm's products or size, but how it markets. Second-track farms sell products through farmers' markets and farm stands and community-supported agriculture (CSA) operations, or perhaps to restaurants or food stores that pay a premium and often retain identification of the farm as part of their marketing strategy. In doing so, these farms often cut out middlemen and reap a larger margin.

Commodity agriculture in Maine has been in decline for more than 50 years. Nearly all of Maine's new farmers follow the second track, what is now called "local agriculture." And it is local agriculture that has generated all the hype. It's responsible for the explosive growth of farmers' markets across the state and for the farm-to-table movement that has transformed Portland, Rockland, and other locations into culinary destinations.

It may appear that commodity agriculture is a thing of the past, while local agriculture is the future. But the reality is more nuanced and complicated. Commodity agriculture not only still constitutes the bulk of the farming in Maine, but also provides the farm infrastructure on which local agriculture relies. (One example: many producers of small livestock would not be able to buy grain in bulk if Maine did not retain a dairy industry.)

Many close observers of Maine agriculture believe that the future of farming here will likely involve an array of farms operating at multiple scales and serving many kinds of markets. We will see continued growth in smaller farms selling through farmers' markets and CSAs, but we also expect that a number of farms that fit that mold today will try to scale up to sell at higher volumes to institutions and supermarkets—where most Mainers get their food.

The key is to scale up in ways that do not diminish the best attributes of "local"—which are not only quality and freshness, but also that more of the financial benefits accrue directly to the farmer. This is the challenge of the next few years. And it's what many farmers and food entrepreneurs are now working on, through innovative food hubs and distribution models.

There's a growing belief that, with the right strategies, Maine can help feed the broader region, greatly benefiting our economy and environment. *A New England Food Vision*, a major study released in 2014, showed how New England could produce half of its own food by midcentury, with Maine poised to lead the way—given that Maine boasts abundant land, plenty of water, handy access to good markets, better growing conditions than many people think, and an increasing supply of capable young farmers.

So farming in Maine is in a pretty good place. It's experiencing growth that's robust, if uneven. And the fundamentals for future growth are strong. That's an enviable position for any economic sector. What lessons can we learn from this?

LESSON NUMBER 1:
SUCCESS RESULTS FROM DOING THINGS DIFFERENTLY.

Most of the farms that are thriving are either new farms or longer-standing farms that have transformed their operations. There is no single strategy for success. In some cases, it's been new products (such as specialty crops or heritage livestock). In other cases, success stems from on-farm processing that adds value to farm inputs, or from new production practices (including growing organically, or using hoop houses to extend the season). Almost always, success has also hinged on new marketing systems that cut out middlemen. And more often than not, a single farm has used a combination of these strategies to succeed.

The common denominator is that thriving farms are producing and/or marketing significantly differently from how most Maine farms were 20 years ago. Success has not come from farms making incremental changes that boost efficiency (though that has also occurred), but from reinventing what they do.

LESSON NUMBER 2:
THE STRENGTH OF OUR COMMUNITIES
IS ALSO A BUSINESS STRENGTH.

I have a theory that one of the reasons that Maine, together with Vermont, has led the local agriculture movement nationally is that both states retain strong communities where residents appreciate their connections to place and to each other. (In a rural town, the owner of the hardware store may support a local farm because that farmer shops there, not at the big box 30 minutes away. In a Maine city, the patrons of a farmers' market not only know their farmers, but often know the farms as well—and cherish the rural landscape that surrounds them.)

The recent growth in farming would not have happened without the enthusiastic support of local consumers, many of whom willingly pay premium prices because they know they are buying more than food. Community support is only part of farming's renewed vitality, but it is an important factor—and one that can be harnessed to support other local businesses wherever strong communities are present.

LESSON NUMBER 3:
INTEGRATED SYSTEMS CREATE SPECIAL OPPORTUNITIES.

Maine agriculture is not exclusively a rural activity, but an interplay between production and use that is increasingly occurring all across the state. A grass-fed beef farmer in Starks sells principally to Portland restaurants. Vegetables from Aroostook County farms processed at Northern Girl in Limestone flow to the Belfast Co-op and the Portland school system. And a wide variety of facilities that serve farmers—a grain mill, a butcher shop, a craft brewery that uses local hops—are popping up in population centers. Urban and suburban areas do more than create demand for farm products: they are increasingly home to this new infrastructure.

Maine is now re-creating the kind of integrated local food system that has not existed for at least 50 years. There is real value in having multiple components of a complete system right here in Maine; and greater value still if that system is spread throughout the state.

The best economic opportunities—and the highest degree of resiliency—may lie in the connections and synergies such a system fosters. Maine will never be in a position to compete by being bigger than other economic players; but in some sectors, like food, Maine can compete by doing many small, interconnected things well.

LESSON NUMBER 4:
GOOD STUFF HAPPENS WHEN THE RIGHT SMALL BUSINESSES RECEIVE THE RIGHT ASSISTANCE.

The growth of local agriculture is the direct result of the hard work and creativity of thousands of individual farmers; but the kind of growth we've seen would never have happened without the contributions of other players. At the top of that list sits the Maine Organic Farmers and Gardeners Association (MOFGA), which has inspired and trained farmers for more than 40 years. Maine Farmland Trust tackles two of farming's greatest challenges: loss of farmland and farm transitions. And financing needs are addressed by Coastal Enterprises Inc. (CEI) and, more recently, Slow Money Maine. Other groups, including a growing number of local groups, make additional contributions.

In Maine, state government has not been as active as nongovernmental organizations (especially when compared to Vermont, Maine's primary local food competitor). But our state government's role has not been inconsequential, with some good programs (e.g., Farms for the Future) and a regulatory environment that, while not perfect, is generally supportive of small-scale farming.

When growing a business sector that barely existed before, this kind of assistance is critical.

A FINAL LESSON

Beyond these lessons, evident from farming's success, we can also learn from the challenges that farmers face. Although farming in Maine is growing, few farmers are making money. Profitability is hindered by current economic realities—and often also by federal policies—that distort food prices. (Though all the trends are moving in the right direction, there is not yet sufficient demand for local farm products at prices that work well for farmers.)

Why are so many farmers willing to work hard for little financial return? One reason is the appealing nature of the work—the ability to be your own boss, work outside, grow things. But another reason is that farmers, better than anyone, often appreciate how the benefits of farming go far beyond economic measures, how farming's ability to rebuild community and improve our planet is worthy of pursuit—even if our current economic system doesn't reward it.

In some ways, the growth of farming in Maine has been in defiance of conventional economic wisdom. Instead, it's been guided by a belief that, in the future, a more sustainable system will, by necessity, not only reward straight economic returns, but also what we do for our communities and environment.

The future of Maine may hinge not just on more farmers, but on more businesspeople from other sectors who begin to think and act like our most forward-looking farmers—who run their farms as if the future they hope for already exists. Maybe we need leaders in other economic sectors to take the same plunge that many farmers have.

The most important lesson to draw from how farming in Maine has grown may be this: that determined people pursuing a system-changing vision can create a self-fulfilling prophecy.

 **John Piotti is** president and chief executive officer of Maine Farmland Trust, a statewide non-profit organization that helps Maine farms remain viable. At the forefront of agricultural issues in Maine for twenty years, he previously managed all the farm programs for Coastal Enterprises, Inc. He is a former chair of the Northeast Sustainable Agriculture Working Group and a former director of the National Campaign for Sustainable Agriculture. In 2005, he was one of eight Americans awarded a prestigious Eisenhower Fellowship, exploring European models for using agriculture as a vehicle to advance sustainable community development. From 2002 to 2010, he also served in the Maine House of Representatives, heading the Agriculture Committee and later serving as the House majority leader. In 2013, he was named to *Maine Magazine*'s inaugural list as one of the fifty people who have done the most for the state.

He lives in Unity with his wife and their two children.

REINVENTING EDUCATION

PREPARING TODAY'S STUDENTS FOR TOMORROW'S ECONOMY

Jim Shaffer and Sue Inches

When public education was first established, its primary purpose was to prepare children for citizenship and work, most often in

family farms or the burgeoning factories of their day.

Now, schools are being asked to pick up the slack for overwhelmed parents, a fragile economy, and widespread stress. In many ways, schools are becoming the mooring and anchor for many kids that the home used to be.

No institution in our society has been more buffeted by the transformative changes in our economy and in our families than our schools. During just one or two generations, we've transitioned from a society in which one parent could stay home to run the family and keep kids from self-destructing, to a society in which there's either a lone parent struggling to stay above water or two parents juggling frantic schedules to keep up. And that's just at the surface of the change that is confronting kids today.

Education, and teachers in particular, do more now to shape the next generation of citizens than at any time before. They are increasingly responsible for producing well-rounded adults, informed citizens, and skilled employees prepared to enter the economy. And despite all of those challenges, we still manage to expect our teachers to possess the wisdom of Solomon and the patience of Job. And, of course, to buy their own construction paper.

Like it or not, the next wave of challenges is upon us, driven largely by the way that the economy and work are changing, and these challenges will continue to push education to experiment and adapt.

> "We cannot always build the future for our youth,
>
> but we can build our youth for the future"
>
> *Franklin Delano Roosevelt*

There are two new ways in which education now has to reshape itself to help Maine accelerate the growth of the next economy. One way is in preparing kids for the new kinds of jobs that are being invented every day. Particularly in high-tech and engineering fields, jobs are going unfilled in Maine because we don't have graduates with the right skills. The other way is about preparing kids to create their own jobs. Today's children, and their children, will increasingly need to create jobs rather than find them.

So this gives rise to the question: How well is Maine doing this? Are we educating ourselves—our students and working adults—to succeed in an economy driven by innovation and entrepreneurship? After talking with dozens of educators and more than 100 teachers and education specialists, here is what we learned.

KINDERGARTEN THROUGH HIGH SCHOOL

In 2011 the Maine Legislature took a bold step by enacting the Common Core Curriculum and a set of Guiding Principles required for high school graduation. These require students to learn the skills needed to succeed in an innovation economy. Those skills include critical thinking, identifying and solving problems, and oral and written communication skills.

The challenge is in changing teaching and testing methods so students actually learn those things. In the years since the legislative action, teachers have been training and new tests have been designed. But old incentives and habits keep many schools focused on "teaching to the test." This results in students memorizing content rather than learning key skills. And because of continued underfunding of training programs and overloaded teaching schedules that don't allow for significant training time, real change will take many years to be to be fully implemented.

But the next economy isn't waiting for us to catch up. Moving into an innovation economy requires a more rapid change in how we educate the next generation. It requires a culture shift. The Common Core, known as "proficiency-based" education, is a 180-degree shift from rewarding only the right answers and equating wrong answers with failure. (Listening to the stories of successful entrepreneurs, it's clear that that many had to accept and learn from failure before they became successful.) If executed well, proficiency-based education can provide students with the mentoring, skills, and knowledge they need to innovate and to add value to the economy and civic life at every level.

Many educators, teachers, and parents realize that an industrial economy model of education—designed to turn out employees who can follow directions—is no longer sufficient. Part of the challenge is to expose students to alternatives. One educator commented that "every fourth grader should understand that entrepreneurship is a career option."

Many are working for change. High school principals are leading the charge of change within their schools. Charter and private schools are experimenting with experiential and community-based education. As many as 50 organizations in Maine are providing after-school programs that help kids learn the skills they'll need to succeed in an innovation economy. A few examples: Junior chievement, Odyssey of the Mind, and First Robotics Competition.

Good things are happening in K–12 education all around the state. But these efforts are fragmented, not universally appreciated, and generally underfunded. The pace of change could be greatly increased by sharing information across school districts and among educational organizations.

POST-SECONDARY EDUCATION

In higher education, we found examples of collaboration among individuals delivering programs, but this collaboration is based on personal networks and is not institutionalized. For example, the Foster Center for Innovation and the Target Technology Center Incubator, both at the University of Maine's Orono campus, share information and resources regularly, because the people running these programs know each other.

But there was scant coordination elsewhere within the University of Maine system. And the highly successful entrepreneurship program at the Southern Maine Community College in South Portland operates in isolation and isn't shared across the community college system.

In the years of budget-cutting and contraction before 2015, our public institutions of higher learning focused on delivering degrees. But innovators and entrepreneurs often aren't interested in degrees. They're interested in how to solve their immediate pressing problems. They want something that the modern economy demands, which is "just in time" education.

In some ways, Maine has been moving in the wrong direction. We've cut programs that are highly supportive of entrepreneurs, including USM's Campus Ventures; USM's Center for Entrepreneurship and Innovation, with its business plan competition; and the patent program at the Maine Law School. These programs served Maine's entrepreneurial economy, and their loss is troubling. The reality seems to be that funding within the U-Maine system is newly focused on credit hours leading to degrees, and not service to businesses and aspiring entrepreneurs.

Even though they don't offer business degrees, some of Maine's private liberal arts colleges have excellent programs to nurture entrepreneurship. Bates, Bowdoin, and Colby offer speaker series, paid internships and practical support for students with an interest in entrepreneurship. College of the Atlantic has a student business incubator, matches students with mentors in the community, and offers an annual cash award to the best student business plan. The University of New England and Colby also offer campus-wide business plan competitions, and UNE recently created a degree in marine entrepreneurship. But like the programs offered by public institutions, these programs are typically only available to matriculated students or alumni.

Optimistically, some new initiatives provide hope: USM has created an interdisciplinary minor in creativity, innovation, and entrepreneurship (ICE), but again, only for degree students. The U-Maine system has also proposed a "Graduate Professional Center" which combines the UMO and USM graduate business programs with the Maine School of Law. This has the potential to offer more value to students who are inclined towards entrepreneurship. But to truly support and nurture an innovation economy, entrepreneurship courses need to be offered across all disciplines, and non-academic entrepreneurship programs (open to matriculated and non-matriculated students) need to be reinstated.

DIRECT SUPPORT FOR ENTREPRENEURS

For post-graduate and non-graduate entrepreneurs, we found an enthusiastic but fragmented "ecosystem" of non-academic support services. These include mentoring and one-on-one counseling through SCORE, Maine Angels, the Maine Center for Entrepreneurial Development, and the Small Business Development Centers. As with the academic programs, any coordination was through the personal relationships among individuals and not due to any structural integration. In 2015, Maine was also at the end of a three-year $3 million grant from the Blackstone Foundation that supported Maine Start-Up and Create Week and a number of other entrepreneurship support programs. This grant was used with great success. As this book was being published, a new collaborative initiative called Maine Accelerates Growth was announced. The focus of the effort is to build a fund that will support entrepreneurship services. The fund will be housed and promoted by the Maine Community Foundation.

So what do we need to do? Let's start at the K–12 level, where we still teach to the test and focus more on content than on skill. We've passed some good laws, but Maine has not provided teachers with the time or training needed to fully understand what it takes to teach a more experiential, proficiency-based curriculum. Leadership, resources, and collaboration are needed to support the good work going on in our schools.

In our public university and community college systems, there are no overarching goals and no institutionalized coordination. There needs to be a higher priority on supporting the *economy* as opposed to simply producing credit hours and degrees.

In general, much good work is being done to prepare students, post-graduates, and non-graduates, to succeed in an innovation economy. But underlying the funding problem is the lack of leadership. Maine's environment for nurturing entrepreneurship and innovation needs an overarching vision and champions who support it.

Maine needs to embrace the preparation of innovators and entrepreneurs—and not just the preparation of students to become task-level workers as a stated objective of education. As simple as it seems, this commitment would have a profound effect on how Maine organizes, funds, and measures the results of education.

Jim Shaffer is a former news media executive who developed a subsequent career as an educator. His 30-plus-year media career took him to Minneapolis, Baltimore, Buffalo, Los Angeles, Chicago, and Portland, Maine. He came to Maine in 1991 to be chief executive officer of Guy Gannett Communications, based in Portland with television, newspaper, and other media properties in seven states. After the sale of Guy Gannett in 1999, Jim studied leadership at Harvard's Kennedy School of Government, which led to an academic career at the University of Southern Maine. He became dean of USM's School of Business in 2006. He retired from USM in 2012, and currently serves on the boards of the Maine Public Broadcasting Network, Portland Ballet, and Envision Maine. He and his architect wife, Lynn, live in Cape Elizabeth.

Sue Inches has worked for many years as a program developer and fundraiser to improve Maine's economy and environment. She served for seven years as director of industry development for Maine's fisheries and aquaculture sectors, and seven more years as deputy director of the State Planning Office. She established the Maine Uniform Building and Energy Code and the Quality of Place Council, which explores ways to enhance Maine's chief economic asset, and wrote the legislation establishing Efficiency Maine. She also served as board chair of Coastal Enterprises. In 2015, she organized and led "Climate Tour: Denmark," in which 14 Maine leaders learned how that country reduced its fossil fuel use by more than a third. She and her husband live on a 25-acre farm in North Yarmouth.

PREPARING THE WORKFORCE WE NEED

Ryan Neale

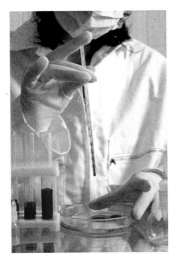

Maine's workforce is vital to our economic success and quality of life in the years ahead. Our challenge is one of both quantity and quality, and the two are closely related: we need enough workers with the diversity of skills and education to meet the current and future needs of Maine employers and create new opportunities for themselves and others in an ever-changing economy.

Maine's challenges are not unique. Developing a workforce with the appropriate skills is a national and global challenge, and the states and regions that are successful will be well positioned in the years ahead. Maine's challenges are particularly tough, though, because of our aging population.

As we've been becoming the oldest state in the country, we're struggling to replace the workers who are retiring. Without a change in that trend, we stand to lose as many as 20,000 workers by 2020[1]

Along with these demographic challenges, the global transition to the knowledge-driven and innovative economy has fundamentally changed the way that many of us work. Accompanying this change is a greater demand for high levels of skill and education. Throughout our economy, we can expect the importance of education, in all its forms, to continue to grow in the years ahead.

---

[1] *Making Maine Work: Growing Maine's Workforce*, 2013, Maine Development Foundation and Maine State Chamber of Commerce.

As one example, jobs that require professional, master's, and associate's degrees are expected to have the highest percentage increase through 2020, and the vast majority of the most promising occupations—those that offer high wages and are in high demand—require some type of postsecondary education.[1]

More is being asked and expected of workers in virtually all economic sectors. The manufacturing sector, long a pillar of Maine's economy, has seen dramatic changes that are indicative of the changes in the larger economy. Productivity in the sector has grown steadily in recent decades, with the number of jobs declining while overall output has remained fairly steady. Repetitive tasks and rigid procedures have largely been replaced with sophisticated equipment and an environment that offers workers a high level of independence, flexibility, and problem solving. Reflecting this change, more Maine manufacturing workers, by percentage, now have college degrees than in years past.

Improving our productivity can help alleviate some of our demographic challenges, and is a key to growing our economy. The makeup of our economy presents some obstacles, however. We have comparatively few jobs in high-productivity sectors like professional and business services. Growing such sectors can help grow our economy and will require employees with high levels of skill and education. Research has shown that innovation accounts for approximately 80 percent of economic growth.[2] Innovation is not limited by industry, occupation, skill level, or educational level; it can take many forms and can happen anywhere in our economy. Entrepreneurship is another key to growing an economy. Mainers between the ages of 20 and 64 generally start more businesses than

[1] *Job Outlook to 2022*, Maine Department of Labor Center for Workforce Research and Information.

[2] *Measures of Growth 2015*, Maine Economic Growth Council and Maine Development Foundation

their counterparts elsewhere in the nation.[1]. For Maine to move our economy forward, we will need a highly skilled and educated workforce full of innovational capacity and entrepreneurial spirit.

We also need to be innovative in the ways that we prepare people for success—the ways by which we provide and encourage the education, knowledge, and skills that help people successfully participate in our economy. All aspects of our educational system need to work together and provide a variety of paths and opportunities for people. If we are to achieve our goals, we need to build and improve upon the connections between educational institutions, businesses, industry partnerships, and workforce training at all levels.

Our economy has undergone dramatic changes in recent years, and the future will bring more change as the economy continues to evolve. Providing the workers of today and tomorrow with the tools they need to adapt to and capitalize on these changes will go a long way toward determining our future success.

 **Ryan Neale** works at the Maine Development Foundation, a statewide non-profit working on sustainable, long-term economic growth for the state, since 2010. He is Program Director for the Maine Economic Growth Council, which works to develop a vision for Maine's economic future and measure our progress toward that vision. He also oversees the *Making Maine Work* report series produced in conjunction with the Maine State Chamber of Commerce. As this book was going to press, he was working on a report on the value of immigration and diversity in Maine's economy and culture. Previously, he worked in the Washington, D.C. office of Senator Olympia Snowe, and in human resources in the private sector. He lives in Brunswick and is an avid skier, hiker, and kayaker.

COMMUNICATING AND CONNECTING WITH THE WORLD

Fletcher Kittredge, GWI

At every stage of Maine's economic history, infrastructure has played a crucial role in our success or failure. The first great infrastructure wasn't something  we built as much as something we found here: our great rivers and shoreline, which gave us the highways of commerce. They allowed cities and towns to grow up; first along the shoreline and later up our navigable rivers all the way to the first natural waterfalls in Augusta, Bangor, and Biddeford.

In the 1840s, the railroads started to become common in Maine, gradually reshaping the state by pushing activity and settlement into rural areas that weren't on waterways. Railroads also moved and reshaped urban areas, as towns like Brownville Junction sprang up and other towns saw their centers move from riverbanks and wharves to areas around their railroad stations. In the last century, highways were built throughout the state and, as before, there were winners and losers. Towns and cities well positioned on a highway grew, and towns that highways bypassed shrank. Within these towns' borders, commercial and residential districts gradually moved in response to highway locations.

GIGABIT NETWORKS ARE THE INFRASTRUCTURE OF THE 21ST CENTURY.

Not everyone wants to live in Maine; our climate precludes that. But far more people want to live in Maine, particularly in rural Maine, than can. They don't live here because they can't find jobs, because they worry about isolation or because they can't build the support network they need. All of these issues can be alleviated by access to 21st century gigabit networks. Advances in telecommunications have always had the effect of shrinking distances ... distances from markets, from the people who provide our services (hospitals), distances from our employers and our employees.

In the 21st century, extremely high-speed internet connection will be the critical infrastructure shaping Maine's economy, business, and population trends. Not everyone wants to live in Maine; our climate precludes that. However, far more people want to live in Maine, particularly rural Maine, than can. They don't live here because they can't find jobs, because they worry about isolation or because they can't build the support network they need.

All of these issues can be alleviated by access to 21st century gigabit networks. Advances in telecommunications have always had the effect of shrinking distances...distances from markets, from the people who deliver us our services (hospitals), distances from our employers and employees. New so-called "gigabit networks" will be at least 100 times faster and more reliable than today's broadband networks. That will open up opportunities that we can only dream about today, as it will allow Mainers to live and work in different places, and help reshape our landscape and population.

For instance, more than 90 percent of Maine businesses are small businesses or home businesses. Even with today's primitive, frustrating internet, many people telecommute. With a far faster and more reliable Internet, cloud computing at home or the small *put*

office could become commonplace. This would/people to work where they live, rather than having to live within a commuting distance of an office or plant. It also makes it more possible for one person to start a new company or sole practice in a rural area, because it makes big company resources available to small businesses via the network.

While today we use conference calls that can be inefficient and frustrating, advanced networks make possible *telepresence*, which is best described as "video conferencing so good it is as if you all are in the same room." Telepresence will make it possible for far more people to work from home, and will enable the delivery of healthcare and other services in the home by remote providers.

Commerce will also be affected by such things as drones and driverless vehicles, which will lower transportation costs, thus making rural living cheaper. In addition, agricultural equipment such as combines will become more intelligent with each model release. Robotic logging, agriculture, and fishing equipment will lower labor costs. Equally important, access to large amounts of detailed data about local conditions on a very fine scale will allow fishermen and farmers to increase productivity with a lower environmental impact. This will also let them automate their regulatory record-keeping, simplifying their lives and reducing stress.

Education is another area that will be affected. Distance education has been growing in recent years, with significant advantages for many students, but also with disadvantages such as reduced access to professors. Improved technology such as telepresence will solve many of those disadvantages and lower the distance barriers, not only between students and teachers, but also between fellow students. This will make it possible, for example, for students to learn about different cultures directly from citizens of those cultures.

Other changes that gigabit networks can stimulate include:

- "Additive Manufacturing," a term used to describe manufacturing via 3D printing. 3D printers are printers that can create three-dimensional objects rather than print on a two-dimensional piece of paper. 3D printers have been around for a few years, but were expensive and limited in the materials they could print in. Both of these issues have been improved in recent years. As these trends continue, we can effectively ship physical objects over fiber optic cables by sending the data completely describing the object to a local 3D printer to be printed.

- "The Internet of Things" (IoT) refers to the increasing number of consumer goods that are connected to the internet. IoT can enhance the lives of the elderly—as, for instance, driverless cars will make it possible to for elderly people to stay in their homes, particularly rural homes, longer. Furthermore, as health equipment such as wheelchairs becomes more intelligent, the date when it becomes necessary to move into a long-term care facility moves out. IoT also improves "telehealth," allowing elderly and sick people to stay in their homes longer by allowing detailed, nonintrusive monitoring at home instead of in a hospital or nursing home.

All of these advances, however, require faster and more reliable Internet service.

HOW THESE NETWORKS WILL RESHAPE MAINE

As we saw from the examples above, networks with superior speed and reliability will allow:

- people to work out of their homes,

- people to stay in their homes when they are infirm,

- businesses to locate in rural areas, and,

- existing natural resource-based businesses to operate more productively and sustainably.

As these networks are built and expanded, we can expect rural depopulation to reverse and rural economies to grow at a greater rate, both through population growth and through increased productivity of rural workers. This is not just a theoretical forecast. Other sections of the country are ahead of us in building these networks and we're seeing the effect on their rural areas. Furthermore, studies between 2010 and 2015 indicate that while more vibrant rural areas attract superior broadband networks, superior broadband networks actually enhance rural areas' economic vibrancy.

WHY MAINE IS BEHIND IN BUILDING THESE NETWORKS

In 2005, Maine had one of the best networks in the country. A decade later, Maine had one of the worst. During those 10 years, there were major investments in upgrading network infrastructure in suburban and urban areas, but not in rural areas. For a variety of reasons, Maine has been particularly disadvantaged.

The Internet is a relatively new technology, only coming into widespread use in the last twenty years. Initially, its use spread by piggy-backing on existing networks built for cable TV or for landline telephone service. Those networks were built using copper wires to send service. While the Internet could and can be reached through those networks, connections always were and continue to be slower and less reliable than over modern fiber networks built specifically for internet access. This problem in Maine persists because investment in these more modern networks has lagged behind other areas of the country.

There are four types of entities investing in building modern fiber optic networks elsewhere, but not in Maine:

1. Telephone companies such as Verizon and AT&T;

2. Cable companies such as Comcast and Time Warner;

3. New players in the Internet world such as Google;

4. Towns and cities.

The first three of these are profit-driven companies that need to put their shareholders' interest ahead of the public interest. For investment in Maine to be worthwhile for them, they need to make more money here than they would elsewhere. Overall, those companies have not felt that it is profitable enough to invest in building networks in Maine. Maine is not a rich state and most of it is sparsely populated. In order to reach the people of rural and small town Maine, those companies would need to build a larger network to reach the same number of customers that they would reach in a city. Some small, local companies have started building fiber networks in Maine, but they lack the resources to build networks throughout the state.

Municipalities, on the other hand, are motivated by a perception of public benefit in investing. Municipalities need to feel that the public benefit of investing in networks exceeds the public cost of the investment. Determining the real public cost and public benefit is complex, and municipalities struggle to come up with a workable formula.

HOW WILL WE GET SUPERIOR NETWORKS BUILT IN MAINE?

Among industry, public advocates, broadband consumers, and technologists, there is surprising consensus about what needs to be done to build gigabit networks to all of Maine, although there are vehement arguments about the details of the solution, based mostly on who gets the money. The consensus is:

- motivate private companies to build to as much of the state as possible;

- in places where private money does not suffice and public/private partnerships are possible, use them;

- in the rest of Maine, provide heavily subsidized or publicly owned networks;

- create a regulatory regime that minimizes the cost of building infrastructure and promotes the above goals.

The state of Maine can make a big difference in all four areas. However, we can also screw things up. Informed and rigorous thinking is necessary before we decide what steps to take. Initially, the state needs to:

- build a neutral, fact-based, non-partisan analysis of our current broadband gaps;

- develop a realistic vision of a world-class network for Maine;

- match its regulatory regime and funding to that vision.

In 2015, bi-partisan legislation was passed that attempted the first of these steps. Unfortunately, all funding, including funding of technical and planning resources, was stripped from the legislation at the last minute. The state agency charged with analysis and funding, the ConnectME Authority, was left weak and underfunded. To move forward, Maine needs a strong, well-funded broadband agency such as those found in many other states, including nearby Vermont and Massachusetts.

Given Maine's limited public funding resources, we need to use our Yankee ingenuity to make the greatest use of private funding by leveraging public/private partnerships. Public/private partnerships often fail to deliver to the public, because the public does a bad job of negotiating the deal and following through to make sure the partnerships deliver the public benefits promised. We can trust Maine citizens to properly evaluate any deal that is transparent and fully disclosed, but there needs to be lifetime auditing when public monies are invested.

Maine has the qualities to build a world-class network—a network that can deliver great economic and quality of life benefits. Let's get started.

Fletcher Kittredge is the chief executive officer of Great Works Internet, or GWI, a telephone and Internet service provider which he founded in Biddeford in 1994. The company has sixty-one facilities state-wide and sells service in all sixteen Maine counties and three New Hampshire counties. GWI is the top corporate sponsor and technology innovation and mission partner for the Maine Center for Entrepreneurial Development in the Center's Maine-wide economic development efforts. Fletcher is a mentor in the Center's Top Gun Entrepreneurship Acceleration Program. As a passionate advocate for broadband growth and network neutrality, he also serves as chair of the advisory council of the ConnectME Authority, a state government component working to increase the availability of broadband throughout Maine. In 2011, *MaineBiz* magazine named him Business Leader of the Year for his leadership of GWI and bringing funding for the Three Ring Binder high-capacity optic fiber project to rural Maine.

BUILDING A RENEWABLE ENERGY ECONOMY
Phil Coupe, Revision Energy

Despite Maine's pristine environmental reputation, the reality is that we have the highest per capita carbon pollution and oil consumption in New England. Salting the wound is the fact that

each year we export $5 billion from the local economy to import fossil fuels from away. Winston Churchill once said "difficulties mastered are opportunities won." While we are often reminded that Maine is riddled with challenges, rarely do we hear about the Dirigo state's opportunities to create jobs, stimulate the economy, and protect our natural assets through the long-term transition to a sustainable and renewable energy-based economy.

History has shown time and again how a common purpose and direction can unleash the power of a group when the objective has clear benefits, such as when Rachel Carson launched the environmental movement with the clarion call of Silent Spring, or when Joshua Chamberlain led Civil War regiments to improbable victories in the face of far greater Confederate manpower and firepower.

Mainers today are in need of leadership and a galvanizing vision for our state and our future that articulates how we can work together to solve problems in a way that benefits all—turning our state's legitimate difficulties into opportunities won.

A good example of a powerful vision and resulting community action is unfolding today in the Pacific Northwest where the Canadian city of Vancouver has embarked on an ambitious plan to become the "Greenest City in the World by 2020[1]." Maine's similarity to Vancouver spawned the idea of turning Maine into the "Economic and Environmental Crown Jewel of New England" by 2030.

The practical Mainer should ask "What is an 'economic and environmental crown jewel?'" and "What's in it for me?" Let's say you started at the Bucksport paper mill straight out of high school 30 years ago and received your pink slip in December 2014.

The slow-motion train wreck of Maine's pulp and paper industry decline has caused much agonizing about how to prevent further erosion, and how to replace the thousands of good-paying jobs and the millions of dollars in municipal tax revenues lost over the preceding two decades. Although there have been emergency funds available to some communities, the state has failed to articulate a long-term strategy and action plan to replace what has been lost as a result of global factors, sending our once-vaunted paper industry down the drain.

In the vacuum of the paper industry's demise, tourism has gradually become Maine's strongest economic driver. Much of our precious tourism industry is predicated on the notion of a pristine natural environment: people with money to spend come from away to enjoy our emerald forests, clean beaches, and quality seafood, not to mention wildlife, remote backcountry, and prime salt and fresh water fishing. Just as Maine's natural assets (forests, lakes and rivers) were critical to the success of the paper industry, these assets have become even more valuable to a tourism industry that stretches from Kittery to Fort Kent, from Bar Harbor to Bethel.

Threatening Maine's $7 billion-per-year tourism industry and its 85,000 jobs is the troubling fact that we have the highest per capita carbon pollution in New England, resulting from a fossil fuel habit that quietly but exponentially grew after the Industrial Revolution. While it is indisputable that fossil fuels have been transformational for humankind—powering quantum leaps in transportation, technology, medicine and warfare —t's also true that we have taken far too long to grasp the existential threat of global carbon extraction and combustion in a closed biosphere system.

Now in the "modern" era, Maine has a fossil fuel infrastructure legacy of more than 400,000 oil boilers heating homes and commercial buildings, heavy emissions from its statewide manufacturing operations, and a transportation sector that contributes 50 percent of the total annual carbon pollution, due to our lack of public transportation and the long distances between our rural communities. Compounding the environmental problem for Mainers is the economic reality that we pay some of the highest costs for fossil fuels in the nation because we have no indigenous supplies to harvest for self-consumption.

Considering our deep dependence on finite fuel resources from away, and their steep economic and environmental costs, do we have a legitimate opportunity to do things differently in a way that will produce tangible benefits for Mainers? Should we aspire to build a green economy as part of a strategy to become New England's economic and environmental crown jewel? There is strong evidence from many countries around the world that the answer is emphatically "yes."

Although Vancouver has only been working on its "Greenest City in the World by 2020" initiative since 2012, early indicators are overwhelmingly positive. Green jobs have increased by 19 percent since inception. Carbon pollution is down by 7 percent. Trips by bicycle, foot and public transit are up by 10 percent. More than 37,000 trees have been planted. Solid waste to landfill or incinerator is down by 18 percent. Air quality violations have dropped by 100 percent. Community engagement is up 1,117 percent in terms of people who have joined the campaign and taken a direct action in accordance with Vancouver's well-defined action plan.

Additional supporting data is evident in the European countries that have been building green economies for decades. Most economists agree that Germany enjoys one of the most robust economies in the world. In the 35 years since Germany launched its "Energiewiende" (energy transition), the country has installed more than 1 million solar arrays and 26,000 wind turbines. On a sunny Sunday in July 2014, Germany set a world record when 60 percent of its total national energy demand was supplied by renewable energy systems. The Germans are at 35 percent renewable energy annually, with a goal of 100 percent by 2050. Would the pragmatic Germans still be investing heavily in renewable energy after 35 years if the Energiewiende were not delivering powerful economic and environmental returns on three and half decades of public and private investment?

The good news is that Maine has abundant renewable resources in the form of wind, tidal, biomass, and solar energy. In fact, we get 33 percent more sunshine per year than Germany, because our latitude is on par with sunny places like Spain and the French Mediterranean. Our solar resource is so powerful that if we covered just 1 percent of Maine's land mass with solar panels, we could harvest enough sunshine to meet 100 percent of Maine's total annual energy demand.

Our steady offshore breeze in the Gulf of Maine has been described as the "Saudi Arabia of wind" based on the colossal amount of available yet untapped renewable energy. Our downeast tides are among the most powerful in the world. And last but not least, Maine is the most heavily forested state in the nation, with 90 percent of our land mass still covered in trees despite 150 years of aggressive but sustainable harvesting, first for ship-building and later for pulp and paper-making.

MAINE'S GREEN ECONOMY OPPORTUNITIES

BIOMASS

Remember the guy from Bucksport, those 400,000 oil boilers (each consuming an average 800 gallons of oil per year and emitting 18,000 pounds of carbon pollution annually) and the most heavily forested state in the nation? With the paper and pulp industry using less wood than it has in decades, Maine has an opportunity repurpose an underutilized renewable resource into clean-burning pellets that can fuel pellet boilers. Switching a household from an oil boiler to a modern, efficient and fully automated pellet boiler reduces carbon pollution by 90 percent annually, reduces the fuel cost by 25 percent, and keeps 100 percent of household heating dollars right here in the local economy.

Job opportunities for displaced paper industry workers include pellet boiler installations, oil boiler recycling, wood harvesting, pellet manufacturing, pellet delivery, and pellet boiler service. It will take decades to replace nearly half a million boilers, creating long-term job opportunities. At an estimated cost of $75 million to get a pipeline started from Boston to southern Maine, does it make sense to expand imports of natural gas from away when we have a cleaner renewable resource right here at home?

SOLAR

Nationally, the solar energy industry added 31,000 jobs in 2014, bringing the total to 174,000 solar jobs across the country—more than the entire U.S. coal industry employs. Most of the jobs are concentrated in states with strong solar policy and meaningful financial incentives, like California, Colorado, New Jersey, Connecticut, Vermont, and Massachusetts.

Since 2003, ReVision Energy has grown from two guys in a garage to become northern New England's largest solar installer with more than 100 employees today spread across four locations in Maine and New Hampshire. Despite general apathy (and pockets of outright hostility) toward renewable energy from state leadership, ReVision Energy is growing modestly in Maine while expanding twice as fast in New Hampshire and Massachusetts. With its abundant solar resource, Maine has the opportunity to grow its solar energy industry by leaps and bounds with just a little encouragement and pro-solar policy from state leadership.

Due to its geographic reach across three states (two of which have strong policy and financial incentives to encourage solar investments), ReVision Energy has the scale and enough favorable policy territory to be resilient in the face of Maine's downbeat policy environment. Meanwhile, smaller Maine-based solar companies are struggling to grow due to the lack of state encouragement. Companies like new start-up Arch Solar, which has developed an innovative greenhouse design that integrates solar electric panels, could be rapidly growing and adding jobs to the economy in a fertile pro-solar policy environment. Similarly, installers like Assured Solar, InSource Renewables, and the Solar Market could be creating new jobs for unemployed millworkers, but instead are in a holding pattern due to negative state policy signals.

Nationwide, a number of factors are driving rapid industry growth, such as the cost for solar electric systems having dropped by 75 percent over the past eight years. As the cost for solar electricity approaches "grid parity" (meaning that clean solar power is as cheap as brown utility power), it has become economically practical to use solar to replace fossil fuel consumption. Modern hyperefficient appliances like air-source heat pumps and heat-pump water heaters are powered by electricity, which can made by sunshine.

The combination of solar power plus an air source heat pump delivers home heating at the cost equivalent of paying 89 cents per gallon for oil, making the investment practical even when oil is hovering around $2 a gallon. In 2015, Efficiency Maine was issuing cash rebates to consumers for the installation of more than 10,000 heat pumps to significantly reduce fossil fuel consumption and carbon emissions.

Electric vehicles are another modern technology poised for mass adoption, presenting multiple layers of economic development and job creation opportunities for Maine. Let's start with the astonishing fact that an electric vehicle costs about 4 cents per mile to drive when the batteries are charged using solar electricity, compared to 15 cents per mile for a gas-powered car of similar size. Plus, the electric vehicle has almost zero maintenance costs—no oil changes, ever. Rotating the tires is all I've ever done in four years of driving a zero-emission Nissan Leaf.

Electric vehicles need charging stations to "fuel" the batteries, representing an opportunity for contractors and electricians to build charging infrastructure for many years to come. Maine will also need about 10 solar panels installed per vehicle to power 10,000 miles of driving per vehicle per year. With more than 1 million vehicles registered in Maine, we have a couple decades of work embedded in the massive project of transitioning from the internal combustion engine to clean solar-powered transportation.

TESLA OF BOATS, ANYONE?

Maine has a proud 150-year shipbuilding tradition, with boat builders still in business today from Kittery to Eastport. Every year, thousands of power boats head out onto Maine's lakes and coastal waters, exacerbating the growing problem of ocean acidification. In response to ocean acidification and its existential threat to our marine fisheries industry, why not build the "Tesla of boats" right here in Maine? National sales figures for electric vehicles show exponential growth month over month between 2010 and 2015, with no slowdown in sight. Instead of sending fleets of diesel and gas-powered pleasure boats and commercial boats to add to all the other carbon pollution, why not launch a clean-boating revolution that will create jobs in research and development, manufacturing, service, solar installations to power the boats, and electric charging installations to charge the boats? Lobstermen are already thinking this way. Today there is a man in southern Maine quietly building his first electric boat to complement the 30 or so electric cars, trucks and mini-vans he has built over the past five years. Could we scale his operation to create local jobs and an entire new manufacturing industry for the state, while simultaneously protecting our vital marine resources?

WIND & TIDAL POWER

Maine's wind industry has contributed billions to the state economy since 2000, but political opposition to large-scale on-shore projects has slowed industry development. The good news is that we have the untapped "Saudi Arabia of wind" offshore in the Gulf of Maine, representing a multi-billion-dollar opportunity for job creation, energy production, and carbon pollution reduction. The University of Maine Advanced Structures & Composites Center is researching and developing the technology that someday will enable us to build industrial-scale turbines to harvest the vast renewable resources just offshore.

Still over the horizon, but likely to get traction before the offshore wind hurdles are overcome, is a global opportunity discovered by Gorham-based Pika Energy. Since 2010, Pika has developed the world's most efficient residential-scale wind turbine. Along the way, Pika's MIT-educated engineers figured out how to make sophisticated electrical hardware and software integrated with wind power, solar power, and battery storage. This creates a micro-grid that can operate in both a "grid-tied" mode when the utility is viable and a resilient "off-grid" mode when the utility is down.

Pika has now patented its potentially disruptive Energy Island technology and is installing the first micro-grid pilot projects with ReVision Energy. This relatively tiny Maine-based manufacturer is in discussions with Tesla and that company's Powerwall battery developers to create a partnership to rapidly deploy the two complementary technologies when they are ready for commercial-scale production. At the same time, Pika is exploring opportunities with global German manufacturing giant Bosch Industries regarding licensing and mass production of Pika's renewable energy hardware and software solutions.

Another relatively small but innovative Maine-based renewable energy manufacturing company is figuring out how to harness energy from tides and powerful remote rivers where dam construction is cost-prohibitive. Ocean Renewable Power Company has already manufactured and installed the world's first grid-connected underwater tidal power turbine, which is making clean renewable electricity just off the coast of Eastport. The company is growing as it develops underwater turbine technology for tidal and riverine applications around the world. Tidal power represents another Maine opportunity for large-scale jobs and economic development. Could we be using tidal power in Eastport and other coastal locations to power zero emission electric lobster boats, bringing economic and environmental sustainability to one of the state's most valuable fisheries?

CONCLUSION

Instead of clinging to our traditional energy sources (oil, propane, natural gas, coal) and historical industries that are declining, Maine has a genuine opportunity to launch an economic and environmental renaissance. Clean energy jobs are growing exponentially in states and countries where leadership has recognized the opportunity and made the commitment to invest in and grow the green economy.

Studies show that renewable energy industry jobs tend to offer better pay, better benefits and better job satisfaction, as well multiplier effects on domestic job creation and economic development:

What could Maine look like in 2030 as a result of an initiative to become the Economic and Environmental Crown Jewel of New England?

Instead of exporting $5 billion per year from the local economy, we are keeping most of that money right here at home to power a vibrant renewable energy economy. Carbon pollution has been significantly reduced and continues to decline, bringing long-term sustainability to our tourism and marine fisheries industries.

Manufacturing jobs have increased exponentially as we build hardware and software for the global renewable energy industry. Our boatbuilding industry has been re-energized and made sustainable for the long haul by innovating electric boat technology. Multiple companies have been incubated out of the University of Maine's Advanced Technology & Composites Center, and they are building the off-shore wind turbine technology that is efficiently harvesting the Saudi Arabia of wind. Ocean Renewable Power Company has achieved critical mass and is now manufacturing underwater turbines to generate electricity from tides and remote rivers.

High-end construction jobs are plentiful as we replace 400,000 oil boilers, install onshore and offshore wind turbines, install tidal power turbines, install solar energy systems, install electric vehicle and boat charging stations, install efficient electric heating appliances, and replace aging fossil fuel infrastructure. This resilient and sustainable economy is producing benefits for all

Mainers by growing the economic pie and protecting the treasure embedded in Maine's natural assets. We are all working together toward the common goal of a sustainable and renewable energy-based economy.

Phil Coupe is a managing partner and co-founder of ReVision Energy, northern New England's largest solar energy company, working to move the region from a fossil fuel-based economy to a sustainable and renewable energy-based economy. Coupe successfully pursued certification for ReVision Energy as a "B Corp," a designation by the Pennsylvania nonprofit B Lab (the "B" in the names stands for beneficial) for businesses that meet rigorous standards of social and environmental performance, accountability, and transparency, increasing value not just for shareholders, but for society. He also serves on the boards of the Environmental & Energy Technology Council of Maine (E2Tech) and Envision Maine, and is chair of Maine Audubon's corporate partner program. Before the launch of ReVision Energy, he was co-founder and director of corporate philanthropy at DrinkMore Water, a Washington, D.C. company which ultra-purifies municipal water to create a lower-cost alternative to bottled spring water. He lives in southern Maine with his wife and three children.

CLIMATE CHANGE:
CHALLENGES AND OPPORTUNITIES

Catherine Lee and Lucy Van Hook

For centuries, the state of Maine has been a leader in the forest products industry, in shipbuilding, in fisheries, and in agriculture. Our tourism industry has been recognized the world over,

and our coastal and inland communities have depended on and maintained vibrant, healthy ecosystems and have been resilient in the face of periodic challenges.

But in recent years, people in Maine have begun to experience a new challenge: the effects of a changing climate. The challenge of our changing climate can seem overwhelming and leave us feeling powerless. However, the need for innovative and adaptive responses creates myriad opportunities, especially when paired with our Maine ingenuity. This challenge and the opportunities it offers us are the subject of this chapter.

CLIMATE CHANGE IN MAINE

Extreme weather events are becoming more common. Maine has had a five-fold increase in the frequency of storms that drop four inches or more of rainfall and bizarre storms with hailstones the size of ping pong balls.[1] Overall precipitation has decreased by 20

---

[1]Mary Pols, "Climate change becomes a matter of mental health," *Portland Press Herald*, September 20, 2015.

http://www.pressherald.com/2015/09/20/climate-change-becomes-a-matter-of-mental-health/

percent in many parts of the state. Meanwhile, we've seen extreme events contribute higher volumes of polluted runoff to our coastal waters, leading to increased closures of shellfish grounds, diminished water quality along our coast, and greater public health risks at our beaches.[1]

The Gulf of Maine, our backyard source of seafood and income to many, is warming 0.5 degrees Celsius every year, faster than 99.8 percent of the world's largest bodies of saltwater.[2] With warming waters, we've seen the lobster population in Maine grow as lobster populations farther south shrink. Rising temperatures are disrupting lobster shedding and movement while causing significant economic hardship for lobstermen along the coast. The mini "heat wave" in 2012 gave us a glimpse of the uncertainty, the erratic harvests, and the adverse economic impacts we could face as the ocean continues to warm.[3]

Air temperatures are going up. Lewiston, for example, is now, on average, 3.4° F warmer than it was a century ago. The ice on Moosehead Lake is breaking up five days earlier on average and maple syrup is running a week earlier than it did 50 years ago. More summer heat waves mean more ozone smog, which is causing damage to our lungs and an increased frequency of asthma.[4] With warmer winters, occurrences of Lyme Disease have increased dramatically, along with three other tick-borne diseases.[5]

---

[1] Judy Berk, Natural Resources Council of Maine, "Global Warming in Maine, Warning Signs, Winning Solutions," 2014. Accessed at: http://www.nrcm.org/our-maine/publications/global-warming-in-maine-warning-signs-winning-solutions/

[2] Rebecca Kessler, "Fast-warming Gulf of Maine offers hint of future for oceans," Yale Environment 360, November 17, 2014. Accessed at: http://e360.yale.edu/feature/fast-warming_gulf_of_maineoffers_hint_of_future_for_oceans/2827/

[3] Kessler, 2014.

[4] Berk, 2014.

[5] Pols, 2015.

MAINE'S EARLY RESPONSES TO CLIMATE CHANGE

Maine entered the second millennium as a national leader in addressing climate change. By 2003, we had enacted one of the first comprehensive state climate action plans in the country. In 2005, the administration of Governor John Baldacci introduced the "Governor's Climate Challenge," a voluntary carbon emission reduction program intended to help Maine's businesses prepare for future regulation of carbon emissions.

In 2006, Maine joined the New England governors and eastern Canadian premiers in calling for a significant reduction in greenhouse gas emissions (10 percent below 1990 levels by 2020), intended to serve as a model for action by other states.[1] Maine colleges were early adopters of the American College and University Presidents' Climate Commitment.[2] In 2009, Maine and nine other states launched the Regional Greenhouse Gas Initiative (RGGI), a groundbreaking program that was the country's first market based mechanism for reducing greenhouse gas emissions. Through the RGGI, Maine reduces emissions and generates revenue, which is then invested in energy efficiency, renewable energy, work force training, and other consumer benefit programs.[3]

So we started out well. Unfortunately, between 2010 and 2015, statewide action on climate has stalled. That's the bad news. The good news is that individual businesses, municipalities, and non-profit organizations are stepping up with innovative initiatives to address climate change, often giving rise to new collaborations.

---

[1] Department of Environmental Protection, "A Climate action plan for Maine: A report to the Joint Standing Committee on natural Resources. December 1, 2004. Accessed at: http://www.eesi.org/files/MaineClimateActionPlan2004Volume%201.pdf

[2] Peter Griesmer, " College keeps carbon pledge in hard times," February 20, 2009. Accessed at:http://bowdoinorient.com/article/4181

[3] Regional Greenhouse Gas Initiative, "RGGI Benefits," Accessed at: http://www.rggi.org/rggi_benefits

NEW INITIATIVES AND OPPORTUNITIES

City planners are installing larger diameter culverts and expanding storm water runoff treatment to ready cities for extreme storms and storm surges. The City of South Portland, in partnership with Garbage to Garden, a local curbside composting company, intends to divert up to 90 percent of all waste from city events to recycling and composting bins.[1] Municipalities are exploring ways to fund weatherization for municipal, residential, and commercial buildings. Improving energy efficiency in city buildings will not only lower municipal costs but also reduce greenhouse gas emissions and take advantage of the weatherization infrastructure and trained workforce stimulated with American Reinvestment and Recovery Act funds. Other cities can learn from these creative municipal actions.

Businesses are developing and creating markets for new energy-efficient and renewable energy goods and services, such as home heat pumps, wood pellet stoves, and energy efficient boilers, along with the contractors and sales forces that support them. Freeport, for example, has launched Solarize Freeport, installing solar panels on more than 40 houses by mid-2015.[2] Maine's budding solar industry is also proposing solar panels on more homes, municipal buildings, and new construction, resulting in more of Maine's electricity needs being met with clean, renewable, energy.

Maine Farmland Trust is working with farmers to plan and prepare for changes in agriculture. Some farmers are seizing the moment and creating water capture and storage facilities for their crops. And some farmers are investigating how they can take advantage of a longer growing season. Stonyvale Farm in Penobscot County has

---

[1] Kelley Bouchard, " South Portland sets zero-waste goal for city events," *Portland Press Herald*, June 23, 2015. Accessed at: http://www.pressherald.com/2015/06/23/south-portland-sets-zero-waste-goal-for-city-events/

[2] Solarize Freeport. Accessed at: www.solarizefreeport.com

installed a manure digester, dubbed "cow power," which is converting manure and food waste into renewable electricity while simultaneously reducing methane emissions.[1]

With warming oceans and increasing uncertainty in fisheries, organizations that support fisheries are expanding efforts to identify new markets for existing seafood products harvested and grown in Maine. The Gulf of Maine Research Institute is studying the impacts of ocean warming, and new species that come with warmer water, and how Maine's fishing industry might diversify to include new and rebounding wild harvest species, as well as new aquaculture opportunities. Last year the Legislature convened a commission to quantify the potential impacts of ocean acidification on Maine's coastal economy. The report highlights businesses that take pro-active measures, as well as ongoing scientific monitoring of historically productive coastal mud flats to ensure future opportunities.

Several Maine forest land owners are generating income as Improved Forest Management Offset projects under California's Cap and Trade program.

One new collaboration is the Maine Climate Table, a broad-based coalition of more than 80 organizations and individuals including representatives from many of the state's key economic sectors—fisheries, farming, economic development, renewable energy companies, faith-based organizations, local authorities, environmental organizations, and many more. The Climate Table came together to engage in collective action to address climate change and its impacts in Maine.

The group is currently exploring a wide range of options for potential action, from a public education campaign to legislative proposals to support for specific projects and programs. Its goal is

[1] Ben McKenna, "Cow power in full bloom at Maine dairy farm," *Portland Press Herald*, January, 20, 2013. Accessed at:

to reduce greenhouse gas emissions in Maine, help communities to adapt and prepare for the impacts of climate change, and engage more Maine people in the effort. The Maine Climate Table is considered a model for state action and represents only one of many efforts to lead once again on the issue of climate change.

This is just a short list of actions Maine people are currently taking to protect our environment and our communities and advance our economy. The need for climate action and adaptation is urgent, but with it comes opportunities for real, impactful responses.

 **Catherine Lee.** Years after a world-opening experience studying in Brazil while she was a high school student in Auburn, Maine, and later becoming a lawyer, in 1997 Catherine founded Lee International Business Development, an international consulting firm that provides advisory services to public and private sector entities interested in climate change.

She has advised developers, sellers and buyers of carbon credits in the compliance and voluntary markets around the world, helping them to evaluate and develop projects, programs, and policies to reduce greenhouse gas emissions and adapt to climate change impacts. More recently, she launched and heads the Maine Climate Table, a broad coalition of individuals and organizations from the nonprofit, business, philanthropic, and government sectors, aimed at creating a model for climate communication and climate action to increase civic engagement and lead to action by elected officials. She is also the initiator of the Justice for Women Lecture Series, begun in 2011 with the University of Maine Law School.

 **Lucy Van Hook** is an independent consultant specializing in climate science and policy, and previously was the fisheries program manager at the Maine Coast Fishermen's Association, working on sustaining Maine's inshore groundfish fishermen. Projects included building a greater constituency and increasing fishermen engagement in the policy arena, business planning, and most recently, engaging fishermen in conversations and management responses to the changing ocean environment. Previously, she worked with Lee International and Climate Focus to develop an approved methodology to quantify greenhouse gas emissions from energy efficiency improvements in residential building under the Verified Carbon Standard, the world's leading voluntary greenhouse gas program. She has been involved in climate change projects since 2005, and in 2015 served on the steering committee of the Maine Climate Table as a representative voice of fishermen and the marine environment. In addition, she is part of a network of Maine organizations working on climate action by augmenting the voices and stories of Maine constituencies already seeing impacts of climate change.

WE CAN'T GROW WITHOUT MORE PEOPLE

Charles Lawton, Planning Decisions

The years since 1985 have brought transformational changes to the

world's economy. The digital communications revolution, the opening of the once-isolated communist economies in Russia and Asia, and the development of resource-rich economics in Africa and Latin America have combined to create a truly global economy.

This transformation has been difficult for all, but particularly hard on Maine. In 1980, Maine had nearly 120,000 jobs in manufacturing, and 34,000 more in federal civilian and military enterprises. Most of these jobs were full-time, good-paying jobs with benefits. And they were scattered widely over all regions of the state. Over the past generation, more than half of these jobs—more than 75,000—have disappeared. And with them, untold thousands more jobs have disappeared in the scores of suppliers to Maine's industrial-era economic base.

While Maine has seen job growth in other sectors during that time—notably in health care, financial services, retail trade and professional and technical services—these new sources of growth have not been as rapid in Maine as in the rest of the country.

Total employment in Maine did grow by nearly 250,000 between 1985 and 2015—an increase of 45 percent. But this figure lagged behind the U.S. growth rate of 58 percent. Just as importantly, the growth that did occur was disproportionately concentrated in the Greater Portland region, leaving much of the rest of the state with even slower growth. In short, the global transformation from the industrial era of the 19th and 20th centuries to the post-industrial era of digital information and international logistics is leaving Maine behind. These changes are unmistakably evident in Maine's below-average rates of growth in

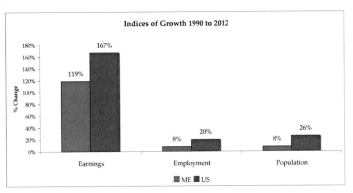

earnings, employment, and population, as indicated in this first chart[1].

Even more importantly, the most recent 2015 forecast prepared for the Maine Department of Transportation to inform its long-term

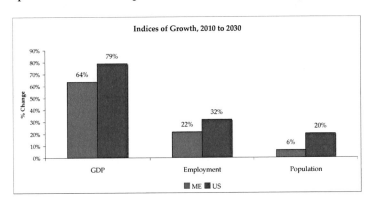

infrastructure planning indicates that, without a significant change in course, Maine's growth will continue to lag the national rate over the next 20 years.

[1] Source: University of Southern Maine, Center for Business and Economic Research.

This lagging growth has severe demographic and fiscal consequences that threaten to make this trend a self-reinforcing death spiral[1]. While all regions of the United States are aging as the "baby boom" generation works its way through the national population distribution, Maine stands out in the absolute decline forecast for its young and working age population over the next 20 years.

According to projections from the Maine Office of Policy and Management, by 2035, the state's population under the age of 65 will decline by 70,000 while its population age 65 and over will increase by more than 150,000.

The implications are clear. If Maine does not somehow generate quality jobs to retain its young and attract workers from outside the state, the current debates, both in Augusta and at town council meetings across the state about how to meet current needs without raising taxes, will only continue and become more heated. [2]

Maine today is at risk of becoming little more than a recreational retreat for day-trippers from the Northeast, a summer colony for the affluent and an impoverished and decaying rural monument to deindustrialization. In the simplest of terms, Maine needs more people. Our economy cannot grow without a labor force to fill jobs, earn incomes and help finance the community-building functions our state and local governments must undertake. This economically driven demographic reality is the most critical challenge facing Maine citizens today.

How can we meet this challenge? There are three solutions. One is to build an entrepreneurial ecosystem that encourages more of our

---

2 Sources: U.S. Bureau of the Census and Maine Office of Policy & Management.

young people to start and grow their own businesses and that attracts entrepreneurs, innovators, and investors from around the country, drawn here by a welcoming attitude and Maine's unparalleled quality of life. The second is to encourage the businesses that are growing in the Greater Boston metro area on our southern border to make their next expansions into Maine, thus bringing high-paying new jobs into the state, many of which are already filled by Maine residents commuting out of state. The third solution is to shed our aversion to "outsiders" and more openly welcome immigrants from other parts of the world.

All three of these approaches require us to become a "welcome center" state, open not only to new ideas but to new people as well.

 **Chuck Lawton is the chief economist at Planning Decisions Inc., a** Maine research and planning firm. He served as the state economist in the Maine Office of Policy and Management, and for six years was a member of the Consensus Economic Forecasting Committee that advises Maine's legislature and governor on economic and revenue forecasting. He also was a professor at the University of Maine at Farmington. He was a charter member of the Federal Reserve Bank of Boston's New England Public Policy Center Advisory Board. He holds a Ph.D. in economics from the Fletcher School at Tufts University. He writes a weekly column for the *Maine Sunday Telegram* and is the author of the book *Maine's Bottom Line: Facing the 21st Century*. His email address is clawton@planningdecisions.com.

WHAT WE NEED TO CONSIDER

Alan Caron

TWO ROADS AHEAD

This is an important moment for Maine. Over the next decade, we will define the state's direction for the next half-century or more. There are only two roads ahead for us. One is a continuation of the road we've been on, where we spend much of our energy trying to bring back yesterday's economy or lure large companies to Maine. If we stay on that road, we'll continue to look to the outside world to save us, focusing on how to attract businesses to Maine by being a cheaper date than other states, or by handing out tax breaks without any strings attached.

It is a road that has taken us nowhere for decades.

The other road takes us toward a new economy in Maine, relevant to the 21st century and driven by our own innovators, entrepreneurs, and smaller businesses. It takes us to an economy where our focus is on *growing* jobs here, from the bottom up, rather than attracting them. And to an economy that is more decentralized and resilient, better able to adapt to future technological and global changes, and less vulnerable to the whims of Wall Street, Washington, Berlin, or Beijing.

Taking that road won't be easy. We'll have to rediscover the spirit of resourceful innovation that has defined Maine since its earliest days. We'll have to let go of parts of the past that aren't returning. And we'll need to find broad agreement on what we want Maine's future to look like, and the steps we must be take to get there.

INVESTING IN OURSELVES

Listen to almost any discussion about growing the economy in Maine and within a minute or two you'll hear words like "attract" or "entice" or "bring" jobs to Maine. What you won't hear much are words like "grow," "generate," or "expand" jobs that are already rooted here.

For about a hundred years or so, we've placed most of our hopes and energy on this strategy of luring jobs to Maine, usually with vague calls to improve "the business climate" or by trying to entice footloose companies to come to Maine for tax breaks and giveaways.

While there have been a few scattered success stories from this strategy, most haven't lasted long, leaving empty industrial parks and call centers around the state. Overall it's been a big investment in time and lost revenues for a small return.

Most economic development people, when pressed to point to jobs created here because of tax incentives talk about the Wal-Mart they stole from the next town over, or the McDonald's that got built, as though those companies don't exist everywhere, tax breaks or not.

This is no small matter. Maine taxpayers now invest as much as a half-billion dollars a year in tax breaks to lure jobs.

Where do all these tax breaks for jobs go? Mostly, we don't really know. Are they creating jobs? Once again, we don't know. But evidence of the failure of that strategy is all around us, in the lack of quality jobs, stagnant population, and an aging state.

This isn't an argument against tax breaks to create jobs. We should absolutely give tax breaks to people who actually create decent jobs. It's an argument against tax breaks that don't produce any measurable results.

The problem is that we give away tax breaks like candy, with no strings attached. We don't insist that promised jobs actually materialize. Nobody checks in later to see what happened and to compare it with what was promised. Nobody measures results. And we have no idea which tax breaks are working and which ones are just money down the drain.

We had a fascinating discussion in Maine, a few years back, which perfectly illustrated how this "tax break" approach to job creation can go awry.

It was a conversation about giving tax breaks to a new company considering coming to the midcoast area. The debate seemed to be over how many hundreds of millions of dollars of tax breaks we should give to a company that was promising to build small aircraft. We eventually lost the bidding war to a Midwestern state that was willing to plunk down about $300 million for the company.

The ensuing finger-pointing about who was to blame for that "loss" barely questioned the company's qualifications or took note of the fact that the market for small aircraft, of the kind the company was proposing, has been glutted for years. Instead, the conversation skipped directly to why we didn't give the company a blank check.

Now that company, in 2015, was months behind in their loan payments and still flying the one prototype they had produced.

Our response to having 'lost' that opportunity pointed to two problems with this approach to development. The first is that people who are too anxious to close a sale seldom bargain hard enough. This is something that every decent car salesman understands fully. If you look like you love the car and want it badly, you'll get it, but at a premium.

Desperation often produces bad decisions, including throwing money at bad investments, trying to be the cheapest date, or believing in something that seems too good to be true.

In this case, the public is hungry – almost desperate – for jobs and will take almost any jobs that sound good, and at almost any cost.

The second problem is the injection of politics into these decisions. When the state hands out tax breaks it is essentially acting as a banker or investor in that business. But most politicians have never worked in banking or investments. For that matter, most haven't even run a business.

That makes it difficult for them to evaluate business ideas and to differentiate between good ideas and scams. When politicians get into this business of tax breaks, it's all about closing the deal, issuing the press releases, photo ops with shovels, and pictures for the next campaign brochure. And it leads to an awful lot of bad decisions.

Politics, to put it bluntly, is a miserable way to run a bank.

And bad bankers don't like audits. So politics has made a bad situation even worse. Every effort to measure the results of tax giveaways seems to run up against a stone wall in Augusta. There's a simple reason for that. Most politicians don't want us to look backward at all the deals announced with great fanfare. They'd prefer to just move onto the next ribbon cutting ceremony and the next election.

Giving tax breaks to companies, like giving out business loans, has to be done by people who know what they're doing, have no self-interest in closing the deal as fast as possible, and make good decisions. It has to be done by professionals charged with evaluating the solidity of claims and verifying results. The further we can separate those folks from politicians, the better.

One of the ironies of the way that we manage tax breaks for jobs is that we expend enormous energy, as a state, worrying about a few welfare cheats, but almost no time looking at where hundreds of millions of dollars go each year in tax breaks.

Should we have invested $300 million in tax breaks to create 300 jobs building phantom aircraft? Maybe we should be asking ourselves an entirely different question. What would happen if we invested that same $300 million in a thousand of the most promising small businesses and startups in Maine, in exchange for each one of them adding one decent job?

In the best-case scenario, that approach would produce 3,000 new jobs, all rooted here in Maine. In the worst case, maybe as few as 300, which is exactly what the airplane manufacturer was promising.

But by investing in our own innovators and entrepreneurs, we'd be investing in ourselves and in the foundations of a more diverse, resilient and solid economy for the future. And we'd be giving our support to our entrepreneurs, innovators, tinkerers, and builders rather than to hazy pipe dreams from away.

CREATING A YOUNGER EC ONOMY

There is a great sadness and apprehension in Maine these days about so many of our young people leaving. Their departure not only robs us of family ties but also reduces the state's vitality

and diversity. We've known for a while that we're the oldest state in the nation, but we haven't known what to do about it.

It's one thing to have older people abandon us for the pleasures of Southern weather in winter. We all understand the desire to flee the icy dark months of January and February in Maine, and it's become part of the Maine experience to welcome those folks back in the spring, usually tanned and grinning. That's all part of a Maine life cycle.

But losing young people is another matter altogether. When they leave the state, we become less energetic and forward-looking. Volunteers aren't as easily replaced. Elected offices go unfilled. Vacant storefronts take longer to fill. New businesses don't start as briskly as they once did. And skilled employees are harder to find.

We've talked about this issue plenty, but mostly attacked the edges of the problem rather than the heart of it, which is a stagnant economy with flat wages and too-few opportunities.

Look anywhere in the world at economies that are growing, and you'll find predominantly young populations that are full of confidence and employing new technologies and innovation. Look at declining economies, and you find places that are aging and resistant to change.

Young people make things happen. It was young people who sailed across dangerous oceans to get here, and survived to tell about it. It was young people who went into the forests to make farms and build homes. And it was young people, by and large, who invented how to live here in the first place.

This notion of young people leaving Maine isn't entirely new, of course. They've abandoned the state for hundreds of years in search of greener pastures or better prospects in Massachusetts, Connecticut, North Carolina, Ohio or California, pushed by cold winters and lured by cheap land or ready jobs.

What's different now is that they're not being replaced by people who are having kids or by younger people moving to Maine. An outflow of young people is a signal flare of a larger failure that threatens us with a loss of exactly the kind of energy we need to reinvent ourselves.

Here's the good news. Young people and entrepreneurs want to be in Maine. This state represents what many young people dream of – a safe, attractive, and wholesome place to raise a family and grow a business.

But if we want young people to stay here and come here, we've got to stop focusing so much energy on the concerns of older and more successful people – things like taxes and energy costs – and put more thought into what young people and other entrepreneurs need to create tomorrow's jobs and lift the larger economy.

As is the case with so many other challenges that Maine faces, the answer always seems to come down to this: focus on the economy, and things will turn around. To keep young people in Maine, we need to build a younger economy.

USING OUR LIMITED RESOURCES WISELY

As a small state with an aging population and modest average incomes, how we deploy our limited public dollars is vitally important. We can't grow the economy without critical investments in education, infrastructure, and business development, but we have limited resources to work with.

We can't raise taxes further without becoming less competitive with other states, making it harder for entrepreneurs to succeed, causing more people to leave and fewer to come here. We also can't increase spending on economic growth without finding savings somewhere else.

Given the constraints we have, Maine is going to need a smarter government to help us grow the next economy. Smarter about how it operates. Smarter about where and how it invests in the economy. And smarter about measuring results and making constant improvements.

In a 2010 book called *Reinventing Maine Government*, which compared Maine's spending on government to that of other similarly rural states, the findings were generally not encouraging.

We spend a very high percentage of our income on government. We've made big investments in K-12 education over the last few decades, which are beginning to show good results. But we spend almost 20 percent below the national average on higher education and community colleges. We also spend less than just about anyone on economic development.

To compound those problems, we've developed a bad habit of attacking a weak economy and widespread poverty with Band-Aid programs that reduce the pain of a weak economy without addressing the source of the pain.

We've also shielded large parts of state government and some parts of both public education and higher education from any innovations that might either reduce payrolls or reshape workplaces.

WE CAN'T WIN WITH A BAD ATTITUDE

People often mistakenly think that the economy is all about math and science, devoid of art or emotion, as though success in economic activity is something that only operates in our heads and never touches our hearts.

So they focus primarily on charts and graphs, government programs, taxes and stock reports. And they overlook some of the most important aspects of any economy, which relate to how people feel about the future and their own prospects for success. By taking that approach, they ignore the power of hope or fear, optimism or pessimism, uncertainty, determination, and resignation.

Economies are in some ways like dynamic living things that include all of the strengths and weaknesses of both the head and the heart. They are a jumble of facts and balance sheets and data that is being constantly churned by ideas and emotions.

It is that mixture of the practical and the emotional that allows small companies with a can-do attitude to defeat bigger ones that are stuck in time. Or small states to succeed where larger ones fail. It was also exactly the combination that allowed 13 small colonies along our Eastern Seaboard to win independence from the greatest power on earth, over 200 years ago.

Fears and pessimism matter, because they hold us back from trying new things. Optimism matters because it allows us to get up in the morning and dare to try new things. Where we are on the pessimism versus optimism scale strongly influences our ability to work with others and sustain morale and teamwork.

In the end, it turns out, how we feel about the future has a lot to do with whether we get the future we want.

If you want to see a good example of all of this at work, pay attention to the next stock market crash or meteoric climb. Ask yourself, while it's happening, if what you're seeing is entirely about facts and figures or if it includes elements of either panic or exuberance. The answer seems obvious: the economy is not only driven by math and logic but also by attitudes and feelings.

What all of that tells us is that to build Maine's next economy, we have to pay attention to not only data and measurable trend lines, but also to how we feel about the future. If we likened ourselves to a large and complex sports team, we'd immediately recognize that no team wins that doesn't believe in itself.

Here's an illustration of the role that attitude plays in economic success or failure that's worth reflecting upon.

In the depths of the greatest Depression Americans have ever known, in the 1930s, President Franklin D. Roosevelt restlessly experimented with any idea that might work to pull us from the brink of financial and political disintegration. He also made hundreds of speeches to get the economy going again.

Of all the things that Roosevelt did or said, none was more powerful or more effective than a few simple words that focused on how Americans were feeling, and their drift toward despair and resignation.

His words weren't about policies or programs, or about rebuilding infrastructure, the solvency of banks, or the looming threats to peace in Europe. Instead, he talked about confidence and hope, which were then under a withering strain.

In his first inaugural address to Congress, in 1933, Roosevelt said this: "The only thing we have to fear . . . is fear itself."

FDR knew more than most, and at a deeply personal level, the dangers of defeatism and pessimism and how they can block recovery and renewal. Struck down by polio at the peak of his physical and (at the time) political power, when he was 39, Roosevelt was never again able to walk without help.

Over a two-year period, he fought relentlessly against the degeneration of his muscles, exercising constantly. Within a year, he was able to walk again, with assistance. Ten years later, he was the president of the United States.

As he was recovering over those first few years, Roosevelt had every reason to succumb to hopelessness and self-pity. A lapse into despair would have been understood by everyone around him. While those sirens of depression may have called to him, Roosevelt instead gathered himself up to go in a different direction.

It is a noteworthy aside that throughout this period, Roosevelt insisted that only optimistic and hopeful people could be around him.

Roosevelt literally lifted himself up on the strength of his personal determination, willing himself back into public life and into our history books. And then he helped a nation do the same.

What Roosevelt understood, as a result of that experience, was that even the best-laid plans and ideas are of no importance where hope and will are low.

A PLAN FOR MAINE'S NEXT ECONOMY

GOLD RUSHES AND INNOVATION

There are generally two ways that economies grow. One is through a fortuitous stockpile of natural resources like gas, oil, gold, timber, or fertile land. The other is from an abundance of human resources and energetic innovators, dreamers, and risk-takers. Much of what we think of as American economic dynamism over the last 200 years has been a direct result of an abundance of the first and sometimes of both.

You might think of these two paths to prosperity as the "gold rush" route and the "innovation" one. "Gold rush" economies occur with any natural resource bonanza that can be easily exploited, often until it's depleted. That is generally the quickest path to riches but seldom leads to lasting or widespread prosperity. Think of abandoned oil rigs and mining ghost towns across the West, or, for that matter, across the planet.

Gold rush economies are characterized by great booms of activity, over a few years or in some cases decades or even centuries, usually followed by some form of collapse, as whatever particular kind of "gold" was found in that area is exhausted.

Since its modern founding, Maine was in many ways a gold rush state. We were blessed with astonishing fish populations in the Gulf of Maine, which is why European sailors and fishermen first came here. Along our shorelines were millions of tons of granite that would end up in some of the nation's great buildings and monuments. Endless forests produced everything from stout sailing ships to lumber for homes and businesses up and down the East Coast, and paper products in the 20th century.

During the height of our 'gold rush' economy Bangor was a prosperous "lumber capital of the world." Magnificent fortunes were built up and down the coast by enterprising sea captains and traders. Portland, before its great fire in 1886, rivaled Boston and New York as a major port for shipping and world trade.

The greatest "gold" we possessed, though, was our powerful rivers. The Penobscot, Kennebec, and Androscoggin rivers, in particular, gave us highways deep into the state. They powered early sawmills to build communities. Later, they would transform the state's economy by producing virtually free power to transport raw lumber to, and run machinery within, our mills.

The Maine gold rush of fish, forests, and rivers went on for well over 300 years before it began to abate, as the "gold" became harder to find or extract. Today, the easy wealth of natural resource extraction is behind us, and we've struggled to avoid becoming our own version of a ghost town of past prosperity.

That has left us with only one choice, which is to take the innovation path to prosperity and to invent our way forward. That is an approach that relies less upon the discovery of "gold" than on ingenuity, skill, determination, and hard work.

IT HELPS TO HAVE A GOOD ROADMAP

If we want to accelerate the growth of Maine's next economy, it will help to have a basic plan or roadmap to guide us. We can 'get there from here' without one, but it's going to cost us time and resources, neither of which we have in abundance.

So what does our plan have to include? First, it has to be bold and transformative. The last thing we need is thousands of small ideas or old notions that we discovered while staring at our rearview mirror, looking at the past. We need ideas that can jolt the state back to life.

Our plan has to reflect who we are and the character of this state. We don't want to become someone else or be like another place. If we did, we'd have already moved there. The plan needs to account for both our liabilities and assets and what we have to work with. And, it should appreciate an essential fact about Maine, which is that real change nearly always comes from the bottom up and not the top down.

But plans are only good when they're married to action. For us to do anything but continue to yell at each other while we're stuck in the mud, we're going to need to come up with a plan that makes sense to a broad array of rural and urban folks, Democrats and Republicans, businesses, environmentalists, and civic leaders. Without widespread agreement on a basic direction for Maine, we'll only continue to meander and drift.

A good plan can help guide our decisions, clarify our priorities and inform our actions. The details of that plan are less important than the overall direction it moves us in, since many details can only be written by thousands of people through their actions.

What we've proposed in this book, so far, is a direction, more than a plan. Focus on innovation, entrepreneurs and small businesses. Grow from within. Create a culture that attracts other innovators. Build from the bottom up. Now, we need more details. But first, let's look at what has already been done, and what we have to consider.

It turns out that there have been countless plans produced on how to grow the Maine economy, over the last 20 to 30 years, so we've got some things to build on. Many are well-written and interesting but lack sufficient energy or clarity to inspire us to new heights.

Others have good elements but seem to lack an overarching vision, other than that we want to "be better" or "be more competitive."

Among the best of the plans we have is an inspiring 2006 report, produced by the Brookings Institution and GrowSmart Maine, called *Charting Maine's Future*. In many ways, the book that you're reading now is the next installment of the part of that report that focused on building an innovation economy.

Brookings argued that we need to focus on a few things, and do them well. They pointed out that Maine has assets that other states and regions would kill for. We have "good bones" in our towns and cities. We have an extraordinarily beautiful natural landscape. And we have a brand for quality products that is the envy of others. They also urged us to get our fiscal house in order, and to build an innovation economy, which is exactly what people across the state, and the people who have written this book, are doing.

WE NEED A PICTURE IN OUR HEADS

When people are required to leap from one side of a fast-moving stream to the other, they need confidence that they can make it. And that confidence requires that they have a clear view of their landing area and a realistic sense of their jumping ability.

Something similar is required for people to leap forward into a new economy. It's not enough to have courage, or the desire to do something, or even the necessity of action. We also need a picture in our heads of what the next economy will look like and the

confidence to jump. Without that, we will never leave the safety of the place where we now stand to leap into that unfamiliar and uncertain future.

Part of the problem we've had in Maine, since the old economy began to decline, has been a lack of vision and imagination about what to do. We don't have a picture in our heads of the next economy. We have fragments of pictures from the old economy – farms and factories, mostly – and pieces of a puzzle about the future. But we haven't put enough of those pieces together yet to see what our future could be.

We can see this absence of imagination in our discussions about Maine's economy. Each year, we ask noted economists to peer into the future and tell us what the next year will bring. We are hardly ever surprised or disappointed now when they tell us it will be much like this one, with some minor ups and downs.

They give us that answer because we're asking the wrong question. We're asking what will happen if we continue doing what we've been doing, or if we do nothing. The only possible answer to that question is that we'll float down the river of change at exactly the rate that the current is carrying us.

The question we should be asking is this one: what would happen if we took bold and effective action, in a concerted way, to grow the next economy?

In order to ask that question we first have to free ourselves of the crippling idea that whatever exists today in Maine is predetermined, or that there is some fixed ceiling on our ability to grow or change. When people believe that nothing they do will fundamentally change their circumstances, they do nothing.

That's what many people thought in North Carolina a generation ago. That state was almost hopelessly locked in some of the nation's worst poverty, stuck in its own past. It was, despite being a Southern state, surprisingly similar to Maine.

Today, North Carolina is one of the fastest-growing and most prosperous states in America, with incomes rising and quality of life improving. They didn't grow because they suddenly found vast new oil reserves or gold in the mountains. Nor did they hit the jackpot in the national lottery for a few big companies that came to save the state. North Carolina dreamed big, hammered out a vision of what it wanted to do, worked together across party lines, made the tough decisions that had to be made, put its money on some big bets, and, over time, transformed itself.

From a state that was largely dependent upon tobacco farming and textile manufacturing – which both succumbed to a changing world – North Carolina has made itself a powerhouse of the nation's economy, ranking regularly in the top 10 in GDP growth and growing at a rate that sometimes doubles the national average.

People are moving to North Carolina in droves, and we should understand how that happened.

Some of that growth was unique to North Carolina's history and culture, to be sure, but much of it wasn't. North Carolina didn't simply chase manufacturing and call centers – it focused on in-state growth first. They supported entrepreneurs and innovators and they got everyone working together, moving in the same direction. They made strategic investments in education, infrastructure and technology, while at the same time working to make it easier to grow a business.

Compare that to what we've been doing in Maine, especially when it comes to "strategic investments in education, infrastructure and technology." In many ways, we've been moving in the opposite direction.

The good news, here in Maine, is that this state is full of people with imagination, intelligence, and courage. What we've lacked is a shared vision and big dreams for the future. And hardly anything good happens without big dreams. Which act as the headlights to illuminate the road ahead. Dreams give us a glimpse of the future and the confidence and direction to act.

Here's one of the dreams that I have for Maine. It's set in a time, just over 10 years from now, after a decade of work to reinvent Maine as a hotbed of new ideas, new products, and creativity – and one of the fastest-growing economies in America.

In that dream, a young and hopeful entrepreneur in a small town in the West is pondering a large map of the country, considering where to start a new company and a new life. She will eventually become her generation's Steve Jobs, growing one of the world's most successful new companies.

She wants to relocate to a place that has a good quality of life and is a fertile place to grow a business. A state that values small start-ups and risk-takers like her, is friendly and energetic, cares for its communities and environment, and values its schools.

She puts her finger on the far upper right corner of that map of America, to a state called Maine, and says, "That is where we should be."

UNDERSTANDING OUR ASSETS

Whether we're trying to build one business or grow an entire regional economy, our 'business' plan has to be built on a sober assessment of both our strengths and weaknesses, or assets and liabilities.

Tons of ink and airtime are devoted to this state's weaknesses and liabilities. By now, virtually any second grader in the state can recite most of them. We're cold, remote, expensive, and disorganized. We could add to that, now, that we're discouraged and prone to self-inflicted wounds.

Reciting our weaknesses is usually where we start and end most conversations about Maine's economy and the future. But no constructive business plan can look only at the expense side of the ledger while ignoring the income side. That barely gives us half the picture.

It turns out that we've got lots of assets. One, as we've mentioned, is the people of Maine. They're tough, tenacious, hardworking and clever. They come from tinkerer stock. And they know more than most about hanging in there when things aren't going great.

Then, of course, there's this place. People who visit us here by the millions marvel at this extraordinary state we live in, with its magnificent natural landscape, colorful history, and friendly and safe communities. We're a place that people love.

And, finally, we have a reputation for quality products and honesty, which is as close to a priceless asset as any business can have.

PROTECTING MAINE'S BRAND

Go to any corner of the country and tell people you're from Maine, and you'll very often get some fond recollection of visiting here, summer camps as a child, or some wish to come here soon.

Maine evokes a powerful and positive feeling among Americans, which accounts for why millions of people visit us each year and thousands of nonresidents own seasonal property on our coastline and lakes.

But the Maine mystique goes beyond good feelings about the state. The state is also regularly associated with words such as "authentic" or "wholesome" or "dependable" or "fair."

The combination of feelings about the beauty and character of Maine, coupled with a reputation for good products, constitutes our brand.

It is a brand that has been built, over a long period of time, by both luck and skill. From the beginning of Maine, as we now know it, we've had two strokes of good luck that are an accident of geography. One is the Maine lobster. In the beginning, we didn't even like lobster and considered it a kind of junk food for poor people. Then we discovered that some of those rich tourists from New York and Boston would actually pay us money for them, and everything changed. The North American lobster, fortunately, just happened to be both abundant and the tastiest lobster in the world.

The second stroke of good luck was our large tracts of forest, which are an accident of cold weather and their remoteness, and a hundred years of paper company ownership that wanted to keep them intact, rather than chopped into small lots or farms.

Those two "lucky" accidents aren't things we invented as much as found. But they became essential to our early brand and its development. If that were all we had to define as our brand, it would make for a lot of nice postcards but not much more.

But Mainers have expanded on those accidental assets by producing a long line of nationally renowned, dependable, and solid goods, and then standing by them. In the 19th century, some of the best sailing ships in the world were built here in Maine, and owning one was considered a source of pride and an indication of success.

Because of those ships, which traveled to every port in the globe, our reputation spread widely. That added a facet to the Maine brand for quality products that were dependable and a good value.

L. L. Bean's history of returning any defective product added another facet to that brand to include honesty, fairness, and pride in our work. More recently, companies like Tom's of Maine, Burt's Bees, Poland Spring Water, and Stonewall Kitchen have added yet another element to the brand, this time for wholesomeness and purity of our products.

Now, a new wave of locally grown and organic foods is benefiting from that brand, and expanding it further.

Does having a strong and positive brand help? You bet. Companies spend billions of dollars every year to get you to feel warm and fuzzy about their brand, their company or their product. They don't do that for the fun of it.

Brand value is so important that in many cases when a company is being purchased, the buyers are more interested in the value of the brand than the value of physical assets.

Aside from the people of Maine, our brand is the greatest asset we have. And it is something we need to protect at all cost. Our hopes for the future depend upon it.

THE PLUMBING AND WIRING

In order to craft a plan for the economy, it's vitally important that we understand the difference between the plumbing and wiring of an economy, without which we will surely decline, and a plan for making us grow.

These two things are regularly confused in economic discussions and plans.

The plumbing and wiring of an economy includes the basics: safe communities, good infrastructure, great schools, skilled employees, and forward-looking leaders. Those are things that everyone needs to do to be in the economic competition. Every state we compete with. Every country trying to take our jobs.

Without those things, no country, state, or community can compete. But having them doesn't guarantee anything other than the price of admission to the game.

Too often, we confuse that wiring and plumbing with a plan for success. So let's be doubly clear: improving schools is important, but it is not, by itself, an economic plan. Nor are better infrastructure or a social safety net or protecting the environment. We need all of those things to prosper, but even with all of them we can still stagnate.

A plan is something that has to include sound plumbing and wiring but needs to go further to differentiate Maine in the marketplace and give us a path to a new prosperity.

BUILDING AN INNOVATIVE, ENTREPRENEURIAL ECONOMY

What does it mean to build an innovative economy here in Maine? Does it mean that everyone is going to be working in high-tech companies or becoming scientists and engineers? Or that we all have to start our own business to have a job?

No, it doesn't. Innovation will be the engine of the next economy. But whatever is driving us forward, people are still going to need houses, office buildings, food, auto repairs, and thousands of other services. There's still going to be plenty of room in an innovation economy for all of the things that we need to keep the state going.

But to bring more prosperity to Maine we've got to bring more resources to Maine, by selling products and services to others and by importing talent and energy. Otherwise, all we're doing is circulating whatever money we have now, which will never allow us to grow.

Building an innovation-driven economy requires us to focus on smaller businesses with two or five or 10 employees that might someday grow to 50 or 100 or 500. That's where most innovation happens. Not that larger businesses don't innovate, or aren't important, but they can take care of themselves. And if we improve the culture for smaller businesses, larger businesses will also benefit.

Building a Maine innovation economy also means promoting innovation in all sectors of the economy and all regions of the state, in jobs from the forests and farms and ocean to computer chips and software and manufacturing. It means bringing innovative thinking into government and schools and colleges, where students are learning to work in teams and to invent products and services and grow their own jobs.

Innovation also has to be working at the community level, with each town and region striving to create their own startup environment, working with local businesses and public and private colleges that are already moving in that direction.

MAKING MAINE AN INCUBATOR OF NEW IDEAS, NEW PRODUCTS AND NEW BUSINESSES

As a small state with a long tradition of small businesses and innovation, Maine is perfectly suited to become the small-business innovation capital of America. But to get there, we're going to need to create an economy and a culture that acts as an incubator for start-ups and small-business growth.

When people think of incubators they often have an image of small enclosures that are designed to help babies grow to a point where they can go out into the world. When we talk about business incubators, we're usually describing an office building or other location where start-up businesses, and sometimes larger fledgling businesses, share resources in a supportive environment.

An incubator state is a different idea. It is a state that intentionally sets out to create a culture, and to build an infrastructure, that will help innovators and entrepreneurs flourish.

For Maine to become an incubator state, we have to set our minds to it. It cannot be just "another thing that would be nice to do." It has to become the centerpiece of our strategy for achieving growth and prosperity.

That means making Maine into a place where ideas, products, and companies that are here now are encouraged to grow. A place where innovators are supported and encouraged to think big, take risks, and even stumble a time or two on the path to success. Where government assistance and incentives are focused first on our innovators and small businesses.

We need to become a state that is not only "Open for Business", as every state is, but one that is particularly open to small innovators, inventors, dreamers, and doers. To become that state, we'll need to beef up our "innovation infrastructure," and build a coordinated and seamless "feeder system" that nurtures budding entrepreneurs and start-ups to move toward becoming tomorrow's success stories.

We have a good start in that infrastructure with organizations like the Maine Technology Institute, Coastal Enterprises, the Maine Center for Entrepreneurial Development, the Maine Development Foundation, the Small Business Administration, and other organizations promoting creativity and entrepreneurship.

Now we need to put that incubator infrastructure on steroids.

GOVERNMENT IS NOT THE PROBLEM – OR THE SOLUTION

Maine politicians have debated what role government should play in the economy for many decades, while the two parties and an occasional independent have played musical chairs in the Governor's Office and the Legislature.

Through it all, and regardless of who was in charge and what their ideology was, we've have one things that's been constant: the economy has never ceased to either rise or fall roughly parallel to whatever was happening with the national economy. If one party was in power when the economy went up, they too all the credit. And if by some stroke of bad luck they were in power when the economy went down, they got the blame.

It turns out that who was in power or what party held what offices has been of little measurable consequence. It has mattered whether there was effective leadership in positions of power, but that hasn't depended on party as much as personalities and their ability to lead.

In the bigger picture, most of what has happened in Maine's economy over the last half-century has had little to do with politicians and everything to do with national boom-and-bust cycles, technological advances, transportation improvements, and competition from places that we never imagined we'd compete with, including our former World War II enemies Japan and Germany, and now China, Korea, Mexico, and India.

But to listen to candidates and political parties, you'd think that government is the essential player in the economy and is almost singularly responsible for our progress or decline. Both parties overstate the role of government, but for different reasons. That has led to a misdiagnosis of the illness we're experiencing and, too often, prescribing the wrong medicine.

That isn't to say that government has no role to play. Strong economies need the plumbing and wiring we talked about earlier. They need honest and hardworking governments that are dependable partners, ensure a level and fair playing field, maintain safe communities, extend and improve transportation and communications networks, and produce an educated citizenry.

But the engines of economic growth, outside of moments of great national distress like the Great Depression of the 1930s, have always have been the people who build businesses and create teams of people to produce winning products. And so it is now.

What we need most today is not partisan solutions but common sense ones. That tend to come from a hybridizing of the best of ideas from Republicans and Democrats, and a lot less taking credit or assigning blame. For that to happen, there needs to be a more listening between the two sides, which is essential to better understanding and respecting the views of others. Without it, the shouting goes on.

Unfortunately, listening is an endangered species in politics today, and the gulf between the two political parties on economic issues, and in particular on the role of government, has never been wider.

So what are they all saying? Republicans seem to believe that government is inherently evil and dysfunctional, except for the military and public safety folks. Their road to prosperity is to get government out of the way by lowering taxes, reducing the cost of energy, weakening environmental standards, and giving away millions of dollars to big companies to lure them to Maine.

Republicans strongly suggest that if it weren't for government, we'd all be gently swinging in hammocks in the Garden of Eden, enjoying fresh wine and dates. Their plan is simple: make government smaller and taxes lower, which will then free up individuals to start more new businesses and expand existing ones. Republicans believe that we can cut our way to prosperity and that spending more money on the things that government does, like roads or schools, is a bad idea. If it were all that simple, of course, states like Alabama and Arkansas would be rich and powerful and big spenders like Germany would be in bankruptcy.

Democrats, meanwhile, have another set of problems. They think government is the way to solve almost every problem. They really don't think about the private-sector economy as much as they should, instead relying upon an unabashed faith in government as not only the protector of the little guys but also the true engine of change and progress.

For many Democrats, the size of the economic pie doesn't seem to matter nearly as much as how equal the slices are. They're content to let someone else bake the pie and then criticize both the chefs and the recipes. Too many Democrats also confuse public spending on "stimulus" projects with an economic strategy. Others still cling to the idea that the best way to attack poverty and hardship is not with private-sector job growth but with more government programs.

The Democratic game plan for prosperity is not quite as simple as the Republican one, but it boils down to this: expand public employment and increase spending on infrastructure, education and training, social programs, health care and on various means to more fairly redistribute resources.

Democrats believe we can invest our way to prosperity. But if larger government produced greater prosperity the Soviet Union would be the ascendant world power today and Greece and Cuba would be flourishing.

That's not to say that either political party is entirely wrong. Republicans are right when they say that we need a more focused and frugal government, that we become uncompetitive when our taxes are higher than other states', and that government doesn't create lasting jobs, except in government itself.

Democrats are right when they say that no modern economy can grow without ensuring equal opportunity for all and without investments in the future, including in expanding education opportunities, safe communities, efficient transportation and communications infrastructure, effective social safety nets, and research and development initiatives.

So what can Maine's leaders do to find common ground and move toward bolder collective action for a new prosperity? We could start with a dose of humility. Nobody — no political party or politician, no economist or school of thought and certainly not the authors of this book — has all the answers. Everyone believes in some things that make sense, and everyone is in some ways tilted too far to starboard or port.

FINDING COMMON SENSE, NONPARTISAN SOLUTIONS

One of the primary reasons why our economy has been stuck for so many years is that we can't agree on whether to go forward or backward, what role government should play and who to blame.

Republicans fault government, deadbeats, the media, and public employee unions, or what they call Democrats. Democrats, in turn, point to greedy corporations, heartless politicians, and the filthy rich, by which they mean Republicans.

But it doesn't stop there. Rural areas blame Portland. Struggling inland towns blame rich coastal ones. Coastal towns blame them back. About the only things that we all seem to agree on is that, somehow, Massachusetts is behind it all.

There are undoubtedly people in government, corporations, unions, and even in southern Maine who bear some responsibility for our anemic economy. There isn't enough evidence yet to place Massachusetts in the conspiracy. While it might be great fun to denounce all of these evil forces arrayed against us, it's also self-defeating. The problem with getting mad at everyone is that we need everyone to pull together to build Maine's next economy.

Aside from the blame game, we're also divided by two other disagreements. The first – whether we should try to rebuild the old economy or build a new one – is beginning to resolve itself, mostly because every attempt to take us backward has failed.

But divisions over the role of government run deep enough to paralyze us from taking any consistent or coordinated action for the future. For decades we've lurched from left to right, unable to decide if we should grow the economy by making government smaller or by investing more in education, infrastructure, and ensuring opportunity for everyone. Unable to agree, we've done both - halfheartedly and sometimes in contradiction to each other - and we've done little of it well.

We've invested in one strategy after another – from ports to highways to industrial parks and call centers – while also cutting support to higher education, recreation and parks, and land conservation. By hitting the accelerator and the brakes at the same time, all we've produced is bald tires.

None of that will change unless we can find common ground approaches to growing the economy, and settle on a few things that we need to do. Here are a few suggestions, for starters:

We could agree that being tight with taxpayer dollars is something that should always happen, but it should apply not only on the program side of government, when poor people are involved, but also on the tax break side of government, when rich people are involved.

We could acknowledge both the limits of what government can do and the value it can bring, by supporting both frugality and smart investments equally, as any successful enterprise would do.

We could focus on and support those things that actually produce results, including tax breaks and programs for business development.

Finally, and most importantly, we could commit to a kind of "save to invest" approach, in which money saved from increasing government efficiency and eliminating ineffective tax breaks would be re-invested in an innovation infrastructure that supports small businesses and innovators, and in research and development, education and technology infrastructure.

WHAT ARE WE GOING TO DO ABOUT IT?

At the beginning of this book, we talked about the most common question that you hear among Maine people when they're confronted with a problem or a challenge: "What are we going to do about it?"

Let's start with the big picture. Here are four over-arching goals that we should embrace.

1. Become a small-business and innovative-incubator state, and a magnet to innovators around the world.

2. Bring more resources into the state by selling more uniquely Maine products to the world.

3. Grow more businesses from within.

4. Reshape education to meet tomorrow's demands.

HERE'S WHAT YOU CAN DO

Let's start with what we can do as individuals and citizens of Maine, and let's also keep that simple:

- If you're already part of the next economy, keep doing what you're doing!

- If you're thinking about creating a new business, do it.

- If you've got an idea for a product or business, pitch it.

- If you're in school, invest at least some of your time in absorbing flexible technical and business skills that you'll need in the next economy, and that will help you to build it.

- If you're an experienced business person or innovator, mentor others and invest in the next economy.

- Become part of a network with others in your community who are working to create a local innovative culture.

- Insist on common sense, non-partisan approaches from your political leaders.

- Share this book and encourage others to get their own.

- Help build a movement for change.

WHAT CAN GOVERNMENT DO?

Kristina Egan, Policy Innovator and Coordinator

Here is a package of ideas that, if adopted together, can strengthen Maine's innovation economy.

The focus here is on strategies that would specifically accelerate the innovation-driven entrepreneurial economy in Maine. We emphasize companies that do this because this is where the majority of job growth comes from, and because these companies grow faster and pay higher wages than the average Maine company.

ACROSS THE NATION, GOVERNMENTS ARE BETTING ON INNOVATION

States across America are making visionary investments that aim to generate long-term paybacks for their economies. Some of the greatest successes are coming from places where the private and public sectors, including higher education, have organized themselves around a particular vision and action plan. North Carolina's successful Research Triangle is a good example that developed from this kind of collaboration and planning.

> **Two thirds of new jobs are created by companies less than five years old.**

Other states are encouraging the expansion of companies poised for growth by offering tax incentives, direct investments, and workforce development. In fact, more than half of the states provide public funding for pre-seed investments, and 40 percent provide tax credits for angel investors. States also fund incubators, small business development centers, enterprise zones, and entrepreneurial education programs.

In the United States and abroad, the economic strategy of trying to attract large companies by offering generous packages of subsidies and tax preferences is falling out of favor. The Kauffman Foundation, a think tank that funds education and entrepreneurship development, says such "smoke stack chasing" is a short-sighted policy and that "a more beneficial long-term strategy is to create an environment that supports innovation and entrepreneurship."

> Offering large companies tax breaks to relocate is not an effective strategy for growing the economy.

Maine's 2010 Science and Technology Action Plan concurs: "Instead of focusing on growing and attracting capital investments in factories and other infrastructure, and trying to compete as the lowest-cost alternative, we need to compete through innovation. An effective "innovation ecosystem" provides supportive infrastructure for new businesses to start, grow, and flourish.

MAINE HAS A NASCENT INNOVATION ECONOMY

Maine has a diversity of organizations that provide different types of financing, such as grants, loans, and equity investments, to different types of organizations, such as research institutions, start-ups, growth companies, and mature companies. These funders include public-private partnerships and nonprofits like the Maine Technology Institute, the Finance Authority of Maine, Coastal Enterprises Inc., and the Maine Venture Fund, as well as private investors such as Maine Angels.

> Building the next economy is a marathon, not a sprint. Maine initiatives need predictable funds at a scale to make a significant impact.

Maine also has numerous organizations that provide expertise and match entrepreneurs with mentors and investors. These include the Maine Center for Entrepreneurial Development, the Small Business Development Centers, SCORE, the Small Business Administration, and economic development agencies. Such organizations also help build networks so that entrepreneurs can learn from their peers. What these organizations collectively lack, though, is coordination or alignment with an over-arching systemic vision.

While Maine has made a good start toward building assets that support innovation, entrepreneurs, and start-ups, we still lack an overall commitment to supporting these as the primary engine of the next economy.

RECOMMENDATION 1:

EVALUATE ALL EXISTING PROGRAMS TO ENSURE

THAT TAX DOLLARS ARE SPENT WISELY

There are three primary ways that the state can help ensure our economic development resources get the most bang for the buck:

- evaluate the return on investment of our economic development programs;

- use the return on investment data to weed out the less effective programs and expand the more effective ones, and,

- improve coordination of the delivery of programs to reduce duplication and overlap.

In 2006, the Maine Legislature's Office of Program Evaluation and Government Accountability assessed 46 economic development initiatives and concluded that the state could be "investing in programs that are ineffective or no longer necessary; spending more than is necessary on administrative costs; or missing opportunities to provide incentives to some businesses while potentially over-subsidizing others." According to a 2012 *New York Times* analysis, Maine spends more than $500 million annually on tax credits and exemptions, loans, and grants to businesses.

Taxpayers should know how well each of these dollars is generating economic growth.

> The state invests more than $500 million annually through tax breaks to support economic development. Are we getting an appropriate return?

All publicly-funded initiatives, whether direct investments or tax expenditures (such as tax breaks or credits), should be rigorously assessed for impact. An independent assessment of all the state's economic development programs would give us information about which incentives, investments, and tax expenditures are working well, are in need of tweaks, or should be eliminated. The key question is: "What should we stop doing so we can afford to do more of what works?" To ensure programs are regularly evaluated, spending and tax expenditure programs should have sunsets.

We should have ongoing bow-to-stern reviews of these programs. Such assessments would allow Maine to allocate resources based on a comparative process that rewards projects and programs with strong track records, or strong potential to contribute to the economy. These comprehensive reviews should be done by a qualified and trusted third party who can conduct an objective assessment using an agreed-upon set of criteria, informed by input from stakeholders. An evaluation cannot be done as a one-off effort. It has to be institutionalized so that it is sustained, like the ongoing evaluations of the Maine Technology Institute and the Maine Economic Improvement Fund, and perhaps modeled on the federal Office of Management and Budget.

Evaluation must also be politically insulated. We need to disconnect investment decisions from the pressure of politics. Because Maine is poorer and larger than the other New England states against which we compete, we have to be particularly disciplined in deploying our limited public resources to the best opportunities to create well-paying jobs, even if this means not dispersing resources to please geographic constituencies. As Laurie Lachance says in *In Search of Silver Buckshot*: "In an effort to be fair, Maine has spread its economic development resources too thin, rendering investment ineffective."

> If we objectively evaluate the performance of our economic development programs, we'll know which investments and tax breaks to eliminate, reform, or expand.

State law requires that economic development programs be regularly evaluated. But limited resources and the practical difficulty of collecting meaningful data present administrative and funding problems. Evaluations need to be thought of as part of the cost of doing business. This cost could be funded by charging an evaluation fee to applicants for the public funds (which is what the Maine Technology Institute does) or by reducing the program's direct investment by the percentage it would cost to do the evaluation.

RECOMMENDATION 2:

COORDINATE ECONOMIC DEVELOPMENT INITIATIVES

As Don Gooding and Eloise Vitelli point out, entrepreneurs need a support network to share strategies and information, reinforce their entrepreneurial cultures, and provide access to cutting-edge thought leaders and ideas. The network includes mentors who can help entrepreneurs navigate challenges and can coach start-ups through the various phases of business development.

Many resources and many economic development programs are available to help entrepreneurs, but entrepreneurs need to know how to find them. The state can play a role in better coordinating and publicizing technical assistance, loans, and grants.

In fact, the state should play this role to ensure public resources are being wisely and efficiently spent. This will reduce duplication and amplify the impact of those programs.

In Maine, we are fortunate to have many committed people and existing resources devoted to helping entrepreneurs, but these efforts lack coordination. In fact, the *Portland Press Herald* wrote, in 2014, that business specialists said "there are more than 300 private and public organizations vying for tax dollars to promote entrepreneurship in Maine. Unfortunately, those dollars are limited, and the various groups rarely work together on coordinated, long-term efforts."

This is not to say that there are not collaborations that have taken root. Mobilize Maine convenes economic development directors around the state. There is a developing culture of networked start-ups in Portland. There was a "coalition of the willing" that came together to push for research and development bonds that included the University of New England, University of Maine, Jackson Laboratory, and the Bangor Chamber, among others. The Maine Development Foundation pulls together economic development professionals regularly. Coastal Enterprises Inc. convenes business owners. The Maine Community Foundation convenes Community Development Finance Institutions, and is now engaged in a coalition approach to accelerating the next economy.

Nonetheless, Maine has a large number of relatively small, autonomous economic development organizations. These include five federal economic development entities in Maine, the state Department of Economic and Community Development, 43 municipalities with economic development staff, and many, many non-governmental organizations providing services. With so many small initiatives, we lose the benefits of a larger scale of operation. One idea everyone agrees on is that there should be "no more programs!" Rather, we need to evaluate and coordinate what we have.

RECOMMENDATION 3: SCALE UP WHAT WORKS

To get new companies off the ground, and to accelerate their growth, entrepreneurs need access to capital. Startups at the pre-revenue or pre-commercialization stages typically need long-term, patient, and low-cost capital, and this often requires public support.

Many of our publicly-supported initiatives are effectively supporting innovation, entrepreneurs, and start-ups. But we have undercapitalized some of our strongest assets, including the Finance Authority of Maine and the Maine Technology Institute. Our strongest programs support the incubation of start-ups, have statewide impact, provide capital to companies throughout their evolution and development, and welcome and attract immigrants and young talent. To help these incredible Maine assets truly transform our economy, we need take these initiatives to scale. To take effective initiatives to scale, Maine can take inspiration from Ohio's Third Frontier bond program, which provides a comprehensive set of tools and resources for entrepreneurs.

The Ohio bond investments are intended to create an innovation ecosystem that supports existing industries as they transform themselves to compete in the modern economy, and to provide support for technology-based companies, universities, and non-profit research institutions. Third Frontier supports incubators, mentoring, intern placements, geographically-based service networks, a suite of activities to accelerate commercialization, pre-seed funds, and loans. This 13-year program has invested $2.1 billion through 2015. An independent evaluation of the bond investment found that "longer-term, structural changes are taking root." Ohio's initial investment of $680 million generated $6.6 billion in economic activity and 41,000 new jobs.

> Let's take the "T" out of the Maine Technology Institute and support all sectors that have the potential to grow and innovate.

We may also consider whether to open bond resources, and other public investments, to a broader definition of entrepreneurs, so that we are not only supporting the seven clusters defined in Maine statute and high tech companies, but also other sectors that have the potential to prosper in our state. As Maine thinks through its focus for these resources, we may want to explore taking the "T" out of MTI, and broaden the focus of MTI and other investments to include non-high tech investments.

Maine should work to develop an appropriate scale and timeframe for these investments as we grow them to a level that can transform the economy. The resources for expansion could come from redirected resources, the General Fund, bonds, and tax reforms. Since building the next economy is a marathon, not a sprint, we need predictable, sustained funds. And, we need them at the necessary scale to make a significant impact.

RECOMMENDATION 4:

INVEST IN RESEARCH AND DEVELOPMENT

Investing in research and development helps Maine compete in the new knowledge-based economy. Universities, public and private laboratories, and industry can generate research that leads to new products, processes, and services. A key to maximizing the economic potential of research and development investment is to identify and facilitate the commercialization of discoveries, and this often requires communications and leadership within the research community.

Investing in R&D has been one of Maine's major economic development strategies. In 1997, Maine ranked 49th in the nation

Maine voters have consistently invested in innovation and small business growth, including:

Annual General Fund investments of $20 - $25 million.

1998	$20 million bond for research and development.
2003	$60 million bond that included R&D for the University of Maine, biomedical research institutions, and more.
2005	$20 million bond for R&D, labs, and career centers.
2007	$50 million bond administered by MTI.
2010	$24 million bond for R&D, historic preservation, and grants to natural resource-based businesses.
2012	$29 million bond for R&D (not implemented by Gov. LePage).
2014	$32 million bonds for new labs and small businesses.

for private and public R&D. Maine's leaders, at the time, decided to focus on changing that rank, and by 2005, Maine had moved up to 35th. However, states across the nation are also prioritizing R&D, and Maine's rank has since fallen.

To close the gap separating Maine from the nation, our research and development investments have to outpace those of the U.S. average. Many experts recommend we triple R&D funding. In 2015, Maine was spending one-third of what state statute set as an investment goal. Funding for facilities and operations should be predictable, stable, and sustained.

> **We need to triple funding for R&D to catch up to the rest of the nation.**

We also can improve the state R&D tax credits so that they stimulate more private R&D investment by making them transferable (i.e. able to be sold on the market), making them available to small firms, and designing them to better complement the federal tax credits.

RECOMMENDATION 5:

REINVENT EDUCATION TO BUILD THE SKILLS NEEDED

The new economy will require that people have the skills to innovate, to be entrepreneurial, and to start and run their own businesses. The state, in partnership with community colleges and the University of Maine System, should work together to better match K-12 curriculum and community college and university offerings to provide the workforce training and skills needed for the next economy. Our educational system needs to do more than train employees. It needs to train people to think and to solve problems so they can enter the workforce as entrepreneurs.

> The next economy requires people who have
> the skills to innovate and start new operations,
> whether as separate startups or within existing
> businesses.

Just as other places have focused on creating world-class athletes (Germany's soccer program, for example), Maine has an opportunity to focus on creating world-class innovators and entrepreneurs.

To help Maine students drive the next economy, we need the following changes:

Create an integrated K- to post-grad entrepreneurship curriculum.

As Tanya Emery at the city of Bangor says, every third grader should know that being an entrepreneur is a career option. The problem is that throughout the K–post grad system, there is no vision, no plan, no one is in charge, and the educators have, if anything, negative incentives to teach entrepreneurship the way entrepreneurs typically want to learn.

Entrepreneurs tend to learn by doing, and therefore entrepreneurship is best taught through experiential learning or a combination of coursework and experiential learning. Envision Maine's Sue Inches and Jim Shaffer have been exploring how entrepreneurship is taught in Maine. Their research reveals that neither academic aspects of entrepreneurship nor experiential entrepreneurship training is a focus of our K–12 education system. Less than 5 percent of students in these grades are exposed to entrepreneurship or small business, and those that are typically learn through *extra*curricular programs, such as Junior Achievement, which rely on teachers volunteering their time.

> Less than 5 percent of K–12 students are
> exposed to entrepreneurship or small business

> in their schools, but more than 90 percent of
> Maine jobs are in small businesses.

There also isn't any kind of overarching vision or coordination of entrepreneurship education within the University of Maine and community college systems. There are some opportunities to learn business and entrepreneurial skills in our institutions of higher learning, but the programs are often hard to find or not well supported by the institutions where they reside.

And, at all levels, incentives do not reward preparing entrepreneurs. At the K–12 level, the incentives are to "teach to the test," and innovation and entrepreneurship are not on the test. At the higher education levels, public institutions are rewarded for delivering certificates, degrees, and/or credit hours that are typically defined around semesters and courses. But this often neglects what entrepreneurs really need. According to Don Gooding, executive director of the Maine Center for Entrepreneurial Development, entrepreneurs need "just-in-time" assistance relevant to their current challenges. This doesn't fit the rewarded model of courses, certificates, and degrees.

We can help prepare K-to-higher education students to become entrepreneurs and small business operators, so that they can fully participate in our economy, by convening the leaders of publicly-funded education institutions to share best practices and develop effective entrepreneurship curriculums. At the community college level, a good model would be Southern Maine Community College's successful Center of Entrepreneurship. At the level of four-year universities, the University of Southern Maine used to have a robust Center for Innovation and Entrepreneurship that directly supported present and aspiring entrepreneurs. However, it was discontinued for lack of funding, because it didn't contribute to USM's focus on granting degrees. Maine needs to re-establish these activities within the University of Maine System, perhaps building on the success of the Foster Center on the university's Orono campus.

Organize higher education as one efficient system. To use higher education resources more efficiently, some fundamental reforms are needed to our community college and state university systems. Maine has six community college campuses and the University of Maine System has seven universities, some with multiple campuses. The University of Maine system also has eight outreach centers, a law school, 31 course sites, and Cooperative Extension. Some people have said that we've sacrificed financial access for our students so we can provide geographic access. The cost of this model is that resources are scattered across campuses, rather than having one center that excels at engineering, for example.

Retrain workers. To help workers in declining industries fully participate in the next economy, we need training programs that bridge the skills gap. We need to expand the work already being done by many organizations around the state, including Educate Maine and its Project>Login. We need to build a workforce with the skills needed for this century's economy.

RECOMMENDATION 6:

INVEST IN TELECOMMUNICATIONS INFRASTRUCTURE

For Maine to become an innovation state, we must improve our telecommunications infrastructure, particularly by expanding broadband access and improving cellphone service reliability. This is just the price of admission to the global economy, and yet Maine ranks 43rd in the nation for broadband adoption. Some 40,000 homes are without fast Internet service, and there is spotty cellular coverage in many Maine places.

The Connect Maine Authority has identified high-priority places for broadband. The next step is to ensure fiber cable is laid to these areas. Earlier in this book, Fletcher Kittredge describes how Maine needs to encourage private companies to build as much fiber as possible, to pursue public private partnerships where possible, and then to subsidize broadband in areas which the private sector won't serve. In Massachusetts, the state matched a federal grant to extend broadband to rural areas in its western region. Maine could also directly contribute funds to match private or public investments to bring broadband service to our underserved regions. To do this, we need a strong, well-funded broadband agency that can develop a vision for a world-class broadband network, and aggressively work to expand broadband throughout the state.

RECOMMENDATION 7:

APPLY THE FULL POWER OF THE EXECUTIVE BRANCH

Many of the above recommendations could be advanced by the governor and the executive branch. In interviews with experts and businesses around the state, we were struck by the fact that no one mentioned the executive branch's work to support economic development. In fact, the Maine Legislature's Office of Program Evaluation & Government Accountability found in 2006 that "There are no meaningful statewide coordination efforts that facilitate understanding or effective management of the state's entire portfolio of [economic development] programs." The governor has a tremendous opportunity to leverage the significant resources and personnel in his agencies to catalyze the development of the next economy. Below, we list some priorities for executive branch action, but in the absence of administration leadership, the legislature could reshape some of these recommendations into a form that can be advanced by the legislative branch.

Reinvent the Department of Economic and Community Development. DECD was created when the economic development paradigm focused on federal block grants. There was general agreement among the economic development experts we interviewed that DECD is not actively promoting entrepreneurs and start-ups, and that the agency needs to be reinvented. In many other states, the economic development agency is a major player in supporting the innovation economy, and stays on the cutting edge by recruiting experienced staff from the private sector. DECD needs to operate with a clear mission for building the innovation and entrepreneurship economy.

Create an Innovation Cabinet. To align public resources, the relevant agencies of the executive branch need coordination. First, these agencies need a set of shared goals. Second, they need high level staff charged with working with the other agencies to achieve those goals.

The administration can lead the agencies in developing these shared goals and hard-wiring the coordination among them. This has been done in many other states, including Massachusetts, where Governor Romney's Office of Commonwealth Development fostered smart growth, and Governor Patrick's Development Cabinet subsequently coordinated the investments in infrastructure, environment, housing, and economic development.

Integrate Entrepreneurship Preparation into K–12 Curriculum. The Department of Education can stimulate and coordinate curriculums that will help our children effectively compete in the next economy. This includes exposing them to concepts, attitudes, and skills of innovation and entrepreneurship. The Department of Education should convene K–12 educators and challenge them to prepare tomorrow's innovators and entrepreneurs.

Appoint an Entrepreneurship Commission. The governor could appoint a commission consisting of high-level representatives of the commissioner of education, the commissioner of economic and community development, the commission of labor, the president of the Maine Community College System, the chancellor of the University of Maine, and the regional chief of the Small Business Administration. The commission should also include K–12 teachers, entrepreneurs, and perhaps the co-chairs of the legislature's Joint Standing Committee on Education. This effort could be modeled on Kentucky's experience in creating a workforce development cabinet, and be focused on developing and executing strategies to build innovation and entrepreneurship skills in K–12 and higher education.

The cabinet would identify best practices across the nation, and create a system to integrate innovation, entrepreneurship and experiential education into our schools, and communicate progress and successes to the general public, in order to facilitate understanding of the need to update curriculums.

Add a 'Start-Up' Facet to Maine's Brand. As mentioned above, the state's marketing resources should be used to brand Maine as a great place to start a business and raise a family. This would help to attract talented immigrants and young people and also to repatriate former Maine residents who are ready to come home. This message should be integrated into the marketing work of the Maine Office of Tourism, and should showcase examples that reinforce the Maine brand and celebrate the many inspiring stories of how our state is building a strong entrepreneurial economy.

JUMP-STARTING MAINE'S NEXT ECONOMY

To jump-start Maine's next economy, we need to be bold and ambitious and to believe in ourselves. Optimistic innovators are currently rebuilding our older businesses, and entrepreneurs are launching new ones. The state government's role should be to support these dreamers and doers by putting our nascent innovation ecosystem on steroids.

We know we aren't investing enough in ourselves. By spending our public economic development dollars wisely and scaling up the types of initiatives we know are already paying dividends, good public policy can help accelerate our transition from an economy of declining industries to an economy of growing companies.

While this chapter has focused on specific ways the government can help support innovation and entrepreneurship, contributing authors to this book have described other things all of us in Maine, including our elected leaders, can do to support the next economy.

George Smith underscored the importance of preserving this special place so that people continue to want to be here and to come here. Our wilderness and coastlines are peerless, and attract visitors and families from around the world. Our vibrant downtowns are a particular magnet for millennials and young people eager to try new things and launch new ventures, and we should continue the many local, regional, and state efforts to revitalize our historic cities.

Charles Lawton and others make the case for being intentional about welcoming new people, particularly immigrants. Immigrants are more likely than others to start new businesses. A "Welcome Center" could ease the challenges people from other countries face when they move here, helping them get settled and contribute to the economy faster.

Cathy Lee and Lucy Van Hook highlight the generational threat of climate change, and how Maine has the opportunity to get ahead of the crisis. We can do this by supporting farmers and fishermen as they begin to adapt their businesses by exploring new markets. We can innovate new energy technologies and products that can simultaneously reduce greenhouse gas emissions and build new markets for Maine.

Phil Coupe explains our opportunities to capitalize on our natural resources and to harness Maine's abundant renewable resources in the form of wind, tidal, biomass, and solar energy.

Maine has the most heavily forested state in the nation; we have some of the strongest tides on earth; we get 33 percent more sunshine than Germany—the world leader in solar energy adoption—and Maine's offshore breeze is the "Saudi Arabia of wind." The state should shape our economic development strategy and projects so that we thoughtfully and aggressively develop this potential driver of our next economy.

There is much that government can do, and much that all of us can do. Let's get started.

 **Kristina Egan** is the policy director for Envision Maine, where she has been the driving force for bringing together a wide array of thinkers on the next economy. She is also a town councilor in Freeport. In her day job, she serves as the Director of Transportation for Massachusetts, a coalition of 40 organizations working to double the number of people using transit across that state, promote walking and biking, and create great places. Since 1995, she has focused on addressing climate change, which she sees as the greatest threat of our time. She started her career in Thailand, working to slow the construction of coal-fired electricity plants by helping Asian countries improve the energy efficiency of appliances, electric motors, and transformers. She subsequently founded a statewide organization in California promoting public transportation to address the transportation sector's greenhouse gas emissions. Egan holds a master's degree in international economics and international relations from Johns Hopkins School of Advanced International Studies.

THE NEXT ECONOMY IS ALREADY GROWING

The next economy has been growing in Maine for a while, in the same way that a young forest grows amidst the older trees. It has been arriving through three waves of pioneers of Maine's next economy.

The first helped to re-invent companies that have been here for generations. The second established a series of highly successful new companies. Now a third generation of startups and innovators is arising around the state.

Here of some examples of the kind of companies that give us encouragement and hope for the future.

THE FIRST WAVE:
OLDER COMPANIES THAT WERE RE-INVENTED
John Lovell, author and journalist

Maine's oldest operating paper mill is an innovation leader. At a time when other Maine paper mills have foundered and closed, a few have been able to refocus on products for which demand is strong.

Sappi Fine Paper's Westbrook mill, built on the bank of the Presumpscot River in 1854, produced traditional paper products for 150 years. But in 2001, the mill restructured to focus on producing release papers, a type of paper it began making in the 1940s that is used in manufacturing products that require a certain texture.

Addressing a 2014 forum sponsored by the Environmental and Energy Technology Council of Maine, the manager of Sappi Fine Paper's Westbrook mill, Donna Cassese, said that "with a 1905 paper-making machine, there was no way we could compete" with newer mills. "But," she added, "it is an awesome machine to make what we make. . . . We do not sell paper, we sell texture."

By 2014, the Westbrook mill was producing 40 percent of the world's supply of "release paper," used to provide the texture on such products as soccer balls, shoes, and high-end clothing. Release paper is 10 times more valuable than the printing and publishing paper the Westbrook mill used to produce, Cassese said.

In the new mill process, a special coating is applied to basic cellulose-based paper "and cure it is with an electron beam," Cassese told her forum audience. "Very, very high tech. This is not your grandfather's paper mill".

According to a 2012 report by Forests for Maine's Future (a partnership of the Maine Tree Foundation, the Maine Forest Service, the Small Woodland Owners Association, and the Center for Research on Sustainable Forests at the University of Maine), the venerable Westbrook mill has become the world's leading producer of release papers used in manufacturing synthetic leathers and fabrics for everything from soccer balls to briefcases, athletic shoes to car wrap.

Release papers are coated with another substance, then the two are peeled apart. Sappi Westbrook's release papers are "printed" or embossed with original textures or designs that transfer to the fabric they're being used to produce.

"Our product is paper. It has a coating on it and an engraved design in it," Cassese told *Fresh from the Woods*, the journal of Forests for Maine's Future. "We sell a roll of paper to a caster, who pours vinyl onto it. Think of the paper as a mold. It's called release paper because you can release the vinyl from the paper and the paper can be reused."

It takes six to eight months to design a new texture and get an engraved roll made. "One of our primary research focuses now is on reducing that," Cassese said. We'd like to be able to do it in two weeks, get the idea, and – boom! – get it out in the marketplace."

In the end, Cassese says, it's all about each mill figuring out what it does well and focusing on how to leverage that for a competitive advantage. "That's what I think is the most s thing for any business, whether you're 150 years old or whatever it is: What are you really good at and how are you unique, and how can you capitalize that into a future growth strategy? That's what it really boils down to."

In 1835, a farmer named William Hussey began making plows in North Berwick. Sixty years later, after a fire destroyed the plow factory, William Hussey's grandsons rebuilt and redefined the company to focus on making fire escapes, bridge supports, ski lifts, and other steel products.

In 1931, the growing family business started building portable outdoor bleachers, and selling them throughout New England. When the baby boom of the 1950s prompted the construction of new schools and gymnasiums, the company adapted its bleacher design for indoor seating, and developed "closed-deck" telescopic gym seats that prevent spectators' feet and personal items from slipping beneath the seat riser.

In 1960, Hussey Seating, as it became known, installed a telescopic platform for fold-down chairs at the Pittsburgh Civic Center, a new and quickly popular concept allowing arenas to provide both seating and floor space for trade shows, concerts, and even rodeos. A few years later, the company introduced an electrically powered system for opening and closing telescopic gym seats and platforms, maximizing seating capacity. And in 1971, the company designed a fold-down chair for its telescopic platforms and installed 3,500 of them at the Augusta Civic Center. More than 1 million of them are now in use around the world.

Further advances and refinements in spectator seating came steadily in the ensuing decades. As Hussey notes on its website, the company "has been a living example of the value of innovation over its history." It has overcome setbacks and crises with perseverance and innovation, turning challenges into opportunities for growth.

"Innovation is often driven by necessity, and the company has used this value in its ability to survive and thrive for such a long period of time," its website says.

On the eve of the company's 175th anniversary, its sixth-generation president and chief executive officer, Tim Hussey, remarked to a newspaper interviewer that the Quaker ethical culture of the company's founders remains strong. "The values of honesty and integrity are attractive to a lot of employees," he said, adding that the culture is one of his favorite things about the company. And with the seventh generation of Husseys coming of age, he remarked that "I think there's something unique about family businesses."

Tennis balls are fuzzy. For that, we can mostly thank a textile manufacturing company in North Monmouth that knows how to adapt to changing markets, surviving and even thriving for more than a century even while many other New England textile mills have gone out of business.

Tex Tech Industries, Inc. is the world's leading producer of tennis ball felt. "Many people outside the business have a hard time believing it's so hard to make tennis ball felt," says Stan Farrell, a project engineer at the company. Needling, washing, dying, napping – to provide the look and feel of the world's best-selling tennis balls, Tex Tech workers do all this to turn raw fiber into rolls and rolls of flawless felt.

In its early years, the company produced fabric for professional baseball team uniforms. Today, in addition to tennis ball felt, it manufactures specialty fibers and fabrics, mainly for security- and safety-related products, such as needled woven/nonwoven fabrics for bulletproof vests and fire protection clothing.

Tex Tech has become a global company, manufacturing more than 7,000 products in its 200,000-square-foot Maine manufacturing and research facility and in other manufacturing facilities in Thailand and China. "It's impressive we've been able to compete in textiles at an international level," Farrell says. "How we've been able to do that is by diversifying into higher-quality products."

And by focusing closely on specific customer needs, Tex Tech's product managers maintain long-term problem-solving relationships with them.

Tex Tech continues to innovate and is researching how it can use its performance fabrics to enhance cockpit door and crew area security for commercial airlines. The company also has a designed fabricated component section, which makes components for other companies, such as wiper felts and cleaning pads for Canon, from Tex Tech's roll goods.

"The vertical integration is becoming more important for Tex Tech by allowing us to provide more value-added products for our customers," Farrell told the Maine Technology Institute in 2015.

The institute has awarded Tex Tech several grants for research and innovation, with which the company has "been able to successfully enter into new markets. Its grant funding has helped us transform ideas into tangible, marketable products."

After earning a bachelor's degree from Boston University, and an MBA and another master's degree from the University of New Hampshire, and several years in managerial positions at computer and manufacturing companies, Carl Spang started an enterprise of his own, using enterprise resource planning software to help other companies manage their businesses.

And in 2007, he put together a partnership to buy Falcon Performance Footwear in Auburn, a small company that manufactured work boots and traditional footwear, and went to work as its president. Falcon soon began developing highly engineered footwear for firefighters throughout North American and expanding into other industrial footwear markets.

From the beginning, Spang focused on quality over quantity, and on relying almost totally on Maine for all of Falcon's manufacturing components. "Chasing cheap labor, trying to make up in volume what you're losing in margins . . . That's not us," he told an interviewer. "Instead of looking at unit costs, we look at total costs. And it's actually cheaper for us to make our boots in Maine. There's an amazing ripple effect when you buy the materials in Maine, employ workers here to make the boots, and they spend their income in Maine. It creates a much more solid economy."

Falcon's expensive, high-tech boots for firefighters were an increasingly good fit with a New Hampshire company that manufactures other firefighting gear, and apparel. So early in 2014, when Spang retired, minority Falcon owner Globe Manufacturing Company became the Auburn company's majority owner, and Falcon Footwear became Globe Footwear.

Roland Landry, a former co-owner of the 55-employee company, told *Mainebiz* that the sale gives the company's workers access to better benefits and a more established human resources department. It also keeps the footwear manufacturing operation in Maine for the foreseeable future, where he and partner Neil Hanley have continued to manage it.

Costing more than $300 a pair, Globe boots can handle extreme temperatures from 20 degrees below zero Fahrenheit to 140 degrees above, are made of flame-resistant leather. They have soles designed for safe and sure footing "in all terrains and when working on ladders," with puncture protection insoles, a moisture barrier, the comfort of athletic sneakers, and certified for "structural firefighting" by the National Fire Protection Association. They can be custom made and modified to fit orthotics or special sizing. The boots have a "running sole footbed," giving users more agility and comfort in tackling various terrain.

Launched as a Maine boat-building company in 1947 by Kenneth Priest, Kenway Boats evolved in the following two decades from wooden to fiberglass vessels, and then to other fiberglass recreational and domestic products, and Kenway Boats was reborn as Kenway Corporation.

The founder's son, Kenneth Priest II, became Kenway's president in 1989 and shaped the Augusta company with a willingness to explore growing new industrial markets and abandon aging ones. Kenway's next president, Ian Kopp, adopted Priest's business philosophy and has applied it with increased vigor.

"In terms of finding opportunity for growth and developing new markets, we have failed plenty at that effort, pursuing possibilities that just did not fit our company well. But with each failure we learned," Kopp told a magazine interviewer in 2013. "We learned more about ourselves, our strengths and our core competencies. We also learned new manufacturing techniques that make us more competitive for upcoming projects."

For example, Kenway Corporation is continually exploring new composite material products and processes, both for strength and for durability and reliability in heavy industrial applications. Much of the company's work involves repairing, replacing, and installing new composite piping, tank and cover systems. Most of Kenway's customer companies are using its composites to combat accelerated corrosion and abrasion problems, particularly in heavy industrial applications.

"The key for us has been to become good at failing," Kopp says. "Sounds strange, I know. But if you fail fast and you fail cheap, then you can devote more time to your opportunities for success.

"For us, what has been the major difference between the failures versus the successes is when it comes to diversification. It is about recognizing our core competencies and learning to say 'no' to the projects that look enticing but just are not a good fit. We're not very good at saying 'no,' but we are getting better."

THE SECOND WAVE OF INNOVATORS

In 1983, a new company in South Portland named Wright Express pioneered a way for fleet truck drivers to efficiently pay for refueling and maintenance stops.

Fleet managers quickly adopted the Wright Express charge card program, and the company built a proprietary network that, over time, earned site acceptance at more than 90 percent of the nation's retail fuel locations and more than 45,000 vehicle maintenance locations.

By 2015, this network had earned the trust of commercial and government fleets with more than 7.7 million vehicles. The company developed proprietary software with which fleets can control purchases on the road while managing operations and reducing costs. It became a global corporate payments company with more than 2,000 employees and operations in ten countries.

And along the way, the growing company shrunk its name. Wright Express – now WEX – has expanded to provide fleet, corporate, and prepaid payment solutions to businesses throughout the world. The company's fleet payment segment provides fleet vehicle payment processing services specifically designed for commercial and government fleets. Its other payment segment provides payment processing solutions for corporate purchasing and transaction monitoring needs.

"Our portfolio of business encompasses a MasterCard-branded corporate card; WEX Fuel Management, a provider of supply chain software solutions for petroleum distributors and retailers; Pacific Pride, an independent fuel distributor franchisee network; and international subsidiaries," WEX says on its website.

Much of the growth has come during the leadership of Melissa Smith, a longtime WEX executive who became the company's chief executive officer in early 2014 and played a key part in helping take the South Portland-based company public. Active in community activities outside her corporate responsibilities, Smith is a marathon runner, and co-founded the Executive Women's Forum, and sheJAMS, a training club that gives women a supportive exercise environment. Joan Benoit Samuelson, a friend and fellow marathoner, says that "Melissa personifies the 'can do' spirit at work, play and in the community," and "has quietly championed enthusiastic engagement between corporate and nonprofit communities in ways to strengthen all of us."

To longtime Maine venture capitalist and entrepreneur Clayton Kyle, the hassle he saw in recycling empty bottles and cans in 2004 was not an annoyance. It was an untapped economic opportunity. So he put together an investment team that purchased the technology and developed the business model for Clynk, a unique, convenient beverage container redemption service.

"In Maine, before Clynk," Kyle recalls, consumers had two choices: Take your empties to a redemption center and wait for someone to hand-count them and pay you for them, or take them to a grocery store and hand-feed them yourself into a "reverse vending machine. "Neither one of those experiences we thought was optimal–and it was the lack of optimal experience we thought was a barrier to recycling success."

Here's how Clynk works: at any Hannaford supermarket, a customer service clerk signs you up, gives you a Clynk wallet card, a packet of matching ID stickers, and a packet of big green Clynk bottle bags to stick them on. Put your bottles and cans in a bag and drop them off at the Clynk station at the supermarket. In a day or two, the value of those empties will show up when you wave your Clynk card at the supermarket's Clynk machine. You can print out a receipt and redeem it with a supermarket cashier while paying for your groceries.

No special trips, no extra waiting, no extra standing in line.

"We realized when we started Clynk that most Mainers are passionate about the environment," says Kyle. "By making recycling easier, Clynk has found that sweet spot where doing the right thing for the environment is also the right thing for growing a Maine company."

Essentially, Kyle has developed a way to streamline the operation of Maine's bottle bill.

The green bag of empty bottles and cans you leave at any of the 46 Hannaford/Clynk drop-off points in Maine is trucked to the Clynk recycling facility in South Portland, where about 200,000 empties are processed each day. Their bar codes are scanned and their return values are credited to the customers' accounts. Glass, plastic, and aluminum containers are sorted and crushed into large bales, and the beverage corporations periodically take the bales away, paying Clynk 3.5 cents to 4 cents per container.

Clynk has become Maine's largest bottle-and-can redeemer and processor, turning a profit on Maine's litter-reducing 1978 bottle bill and creating jobs while providing a valuable service to both beverage consumers and retailers.

"Because we've made it really easy for people to recycle, and since our operation is highly streamlined, the company has thrived in just a few years of operation," says Kyle. "By sharing the costs of collection and sorting with beverage distributors, our company has had room to create a lean and efficient system that works well for Maine."

Maine 1st Congressional District Representative Chellie Pingree can remember when IDEXX Laboratories, Inc., founded in 1983, was a five-employee operation on the Portland waterfront when she was a farmer, taking livestock blood samples there for research.

The company began with diagnostic kits and computerized monitoring systems for poultry, cattle and swine producers, and soon expanded to producing devices to test dogs and cats for illnesses.

In Westbrook three decades later, IDEXX had become the global market leader in diagnostics and information technology solutions for animal health and water and milk quality, providing 50,000 veterinary clinics worldwide with diagnostic and information technology-based products and services.

Along the way, IDEXX bought the research and diagnostic laboratory business of the University of Missouri's College of Veterinary Medicine in 2011, and in 2013 bought the company in Brazil that distributes its testing products there.

In 2014, the growing pet diagnostic and technology company unveiled a $35 million, high-efficiency expansion that reflected its continued global growth, with about 2,100 employees in Maine and about 3,800 in the rest of the world. The new building added 107,700 square feet to the headquarters of Maine's largest publicly traded company. The expansion came on the heels of a decade in which IDEXX increased its Maine workforce from around 800 employees to about 1,800, and completed an $80 million of renovation and new construction of its home base.

The company's president and chief executive officer, Jonathan Ayers, attributes IDEXX's growth to strong research and development, and new products he says lead the market. "It's like Apple created the iPhone and the iPod," he told an interviewer at the time. "The stuff we sell today didn't exist before we launched it."

The company's plastic Snap 4Dx device, for example, is 2½ inches long with a trough at one end to catch blood and a testing strip that changes color to indicate whether a pet has one of four diseases, including heartworm and Lyme disease (which Ayers said used to require thorough lab work to detect). "You put blood into it, and if the dots light up, you have a disease." Each year, IDEXX produces 26 million of them.

Corson "Corky" Ellis and his wife, Marion, a former New York bond trader, and their two pre-teen children, had grown tired of living in New Jersey with its traffic and crowds and pollution. Wanting "to try living in a cleaner place . . . a simpler life," he told an interviewer, they moved to Maine in 1995.

With an English degree from Amherst College and an MBA from Columbia University, Ellis launched a software company in

Yarmouth. His enterprise, Kepware Technologies, developed a portfolio of software that lets disparate industrial machinery communicate. Soon, Kepware began to grow, and moved into larger office space in nearby Portland.

The company's software products evolved to fill critical needs of companies throughout the world, ranging from pharmaceutical clean rooms, to auto plants, to oil rigs and pipelines, to meat packing facilities and beyond. For example, a 2,700-acre vineyard uses Kepware software to monitor and control its irrigation system, which includes solar-powered flow meters, pumps, alarms, and personal computers.

But Ellis found a problem with his company's growth: a shortage of prospective employees. "In 2002," he told an interviewer, "we couldn't find programmers, so we went to the University of Maine and asked: why are we not getting people to apply? We ended up starting three $8,000 scholarships and have four summer internship programs."

Ellis also became involved in efforts to improve education in Maine. "We see technology education as the key to creating a technology economy in Maine. We need to go into the high schools here. We need more engineers. Maine graduates 60 electrical and mechanical engineers a year . . . should be triple that."

Kepware donated 36 of its software licenses, worth $36,000, to the University of Maine so students could familiarize themselves with the software and its uses. The company invested in the university by establishing three computer technology scholarships of $7,500 each. It also supports state robotics competitions, with Ellis serving on the board of the Robotics Institute of Maine. Ellis came to believe that Maine's science-based businesses to connect their workplace needs with Maine's public school math and science teachers.

Assuming the post of company chairman in 2014 allowed Ellis to focus more attention on Maine's long-range education needs, and allowed his junior partner, Tony Paine, who joined the company as an engineer in 1996, to become Kenway Technology's chief executive officer. Paine was replaced as the company's president by fellow engineer Brett Austin, who told an interviewer later in 2014 that "we have the benefit of being in a space where a massive amount of data is being produced, and it's growing every day."

STONEWALL KITCHEN
Creators of Specialty Foods

Jon King and Jim Stott had a garden, and they both loved to cook. They made jars of jams, jellies, pickled vegetables, and mustards in their kitchen as low-cost holiday gifts for their friends and families and friends.

When King took some of his jams and vinegars to his day job at a greenhouse, a coworker told him about an opening at the Portsmouth Seacoast Growers Association Farmers Market. The market was limited to 15 vendors, and vacancies were rare. King and Stott jumped on it.

Stott later told an online magazine that they had 10 minutes to come up with a name and fill out the forms. Sitting at their kitchen table, "We jotted down a list of everything we thought of. 'Jim and Jon's Jams and Jellies' was one of the options. We would not be here if we went with that. It was March, and it was snowing, and there was a stone wall right outside the kitchen window. This old stone wall with a little spattering of snow – I thought it would make a great graphic." They wrote it on the form, and in 1991, Stonewall Kitchen was born. And soon afterward, when a businesswoman stopped at their market table and bought every jar, they realized they were in the wholesale business.

Two years later, national retailer Crate & Barrel approached them with an order for 2,500 jars of their orange cranberry marmalade, which took them a month to make. It was time to increase production capacity, so they bought a barn in Kittery.

By 1999, Stonewall Kitchen's momentum required a new and bigger facility. King and Stott bought an eight-acre parcel in nearby York and built a 46,000-square foot headquarters. In subsequent years, they added 5,200 square feet of office space, a lunch bistro and a cooking school, and a shop to sell their jam-and-jelly mainstays, grille sauces, mustards, chutneys, pancake mixes and dessert sauces, as well as kitchen tools, place settings, and home decor items.

By 2015, Stonewall Kitchen had more than 6,000 wholesale accounts nationwide, thriving catalog and web divisions, 11 retail company stores along the East Coast, and a staff growing into the hundreds. And it was time, King and Stott decided, to retire.

So they hired an investment banker to find a buyer, and sold their enterprise to a private equity firm with offices in New York City and Los Angeles. King decided to stay for three years as chief creative officer. "We've worked so hard to create this brand," he told the *Portland Press Herald*. "The one thing we didn't want to do is stagnate. We didn't want to deprive the company of the opportunity to grow. But we knew we weren't the ones who wanted to do that alone."

Particle Analysis with Vision
FLUID IMAGING TECHNOLOGIES, INC.

Christian Sieracki, an engineer with a PhD in optical physics, had an idea: an image-based fluid cells and particles analysis instrument that he had developed at the Bigelow Laboratory for Ocean Science in Boothbay Harbor could be licensed and marketed.

Kent Peterson, an accomplished corporate chief executive officer, also had an idea: Sieracki's device could be marketed worldwide, and not just to scientists.

They formed a company, Fluid Imaging Technologies, to further develop the instrument, naming it the FlowCAM. Originally invented to study plankton in ocean water, the instrument proved to have wider applications.

"I was convinced that the fundamental core competency of digital imaging flow cytometry, as well as digital imaging particle analysis, was a technology that the market badly needed," Peterson said after Sieracki recruited him in 1999. "I realized it has a big place in manufacturing research. Existing methods were slow and labor-intensive, so relatively little data could be developed in a reasonable amount of time. That was when I decided to go all in, and facilitate the growth of this business."

At first, their new company sold FlowCAMs exclusively to oceanographic institutes and universities. But within a few years, Fluid Imaging Technologies also had industrial customers. FIT outgrew its attic-over-a-garage facilities in Edgecomb, near Boothbay, and moved to larger space in Yarmouth.

"Since our founding, we have been the world-leader in particle analysis instrumentation based upon digital imaging technology, the company says on its website. "Our flagship product, FlowCAM, was the first imaging particle analyzer on the market, and continues to lead the way in hardware innovations."

In mid-2013, with expanding sales and expanding staff – customer support, product development and engineering, laboratory services, and manufacturing and production, as well as sales, marketing, administration, and senior management – Fluid Imaging outgrew its Yarmouth space and moved to a new, 18,000-square-foot space in

Scarborough with a better testing laboratory and bigger production capability.

Going far beyond its initial use in oceanographic research, the FlowCAM can now used in the production of petrochemicals, pharmaceuticals, food, cosmetics, and photocopier toner. A dishwasher manufacturer, for example, can use the FlowCAM to measure how clean the wastewater is from its newest dishwasher model. "There's no limit to the practical applications," Peterson says.

In 1968, Tom Chappell left an insurance company job in Philadelphia and moved with his wife, Kate, to Kennebunk, Maine, and joined his father's fledgling chemical business in Biddeford. Two years later, he borrowed $5,000 and began making a non-caustic, phosphate-free laundry detergent marketed in recyclable jugs. Within a year, he and Kate were turning a profit and rejecting buyout offers. Five more years later, their company had a new name – Tom's of Maine – and a new product: America's first all-natural toothpaste.

Epitomizing the concept of doing well by doing good, Chappell built his socially responsible business by producing wholesome personal care products made entirely from all-natural ingredients. Tom's of Maine grew and grew, but Chappell's material side was increasingly overshadowed by his spiritual side, and so it came to pass that he enrolled in Harvard Divinity School, saying after his 1991 graduation that he had learned to make "systematic studies of philosophy and ethical business practices."

In one of the company's subsequent annual reports, Chappell wrote that "the ultimate is, of course, that of the common good, a goal that is beyond our private hopes. The common good is Tom's of Maine's ultimate reason for being; the private goods are accomplished along the way."

In 2006, Tom and Kate Chappell sold a controlling stake in their company to Colgate-Palmolive for $100 million, with the stipulation that the policies and company culture of the Tom's of Maine brand remain in place.

Along the way, Tom's of Maine made numerous grants to nonprofit groups and projects serving the environment, the arts, human needs, education, and Native American interests. The company also encouraged employees to devote some of their paid company time to working for nonprofit causes and enterprises.

Before the sale, Chappell told a magazine interviewer that "we really are operating in the middle of a paradox – basically, learning how to celebrate both love and profit, to serve both God and Mammon, to be both acquirers and givers."

While working as an engineer, installing computer systems for ABB, an automation technology company, John Coleman realized he preferred marketing and earned an MBA. In 1993, he and the company's creative director decided to launch an advertising agency in Portland and ask ABB for its business, and the company agreed. "I woke up one day running an ad agency and had never stepped foot in one," Coleman recalled later.

He named the agency "The VIA Agency," for "Vision, Instinct, Action."

In its first decade, VIA undertook brand positioning, website development, and business-to-business campaigns for a few global technology companies. For the next decade and a half, the agency operated largely as a brand strategy and interactive firm, and began pushing to become nationally known.

At the same time, the Maine College of Art had been trying to sell the Baxter Building, an aging downtown structure that had for many years housed the city's library, and later, art classrooms. Coleman was drawn to it. Rationally, he knew buying it might not be a good idea. Emotionally, he felt that an ad agency would be the former library's spiritual descendant. And clients would be impressed by the building's Romanesque façade and cavernous interior. So in 2010, it became VIA's new home.

During the next two years, the strategic and analytical ad agency got more creative, and got more big clients, including Perdue chicken, Friendly's restaurants, Romano's Macaroni Grill, Prestige Brands, and People's United Bank. Revenue rose by more than 20 percent in 2010 and 35 percent in 2011.

"We want to be the first agency to truly bring exceptionally strategically driven work at the highest-quality creative levels," Coleman said at the time. Other ad agencies, he said, tend to be one or the other.

In 2012, Coleman hired a new president, Leeann Leahy, to "help take the shop to the next level. . . . We hired Leeann away from Madison Avenue and New York City because she had a vision into what brands are looking for and what advertising professionals want in an employer. Under her leadership, the VIA Agency has grown into a coveted, creative destination for the nation's top companies and the industry's leading professionals."

Beyond the new business, Leahy instituted such quirky agency features as a sabbatical program and "Free Beer & Fiction nights," which may have led *AdAge* to call VIA one of the "40 best places to work in advertising and media" for 2014.

And the first thing Coleman did as VIA's new chairman was to give the agency to its employees, transferring his shares to them as part of an incentive program.

In April 2014, the magazine *Men's Health* ranked 100 American cities according to their coffee consumption: the percentage of households that own coffeemakers and buy coffee; the household average spent on coffee; coffee shops per capita; percentage of people who drink coffee and who drink at least five cups a day. Number 1 on the list: Portland, Maine.

A popular Portland coffee enterprise, Coffee By Design, may have contributed to Portland's top score.

Founders Mary Allen Lindemann and her husband, Alan Spear, launched their first café in 1994, focusing on their dual passions of coffee and community. Twenty years later, the couple's enterprise had grown to 55 employees, five cafés, and an expanded roasting facility. The company also sells nearly half a million pounds of coffee beans a year through about 300 retailers as far away as Las Vegas.

The "community" part of the couple's focus means Coffee By Design supports local arts and nonprofit groups. A dollar for each pound of their Rebel Blend, for example, is funneled to community arts funding, and the couple co-founded Portland Buy Local and First Friday Artwalk.

On their business website, Lindemann and Spear say that "Coffee By Design doesn't believe bigger is better. We believe that being selective is better, and therefore only choose to work with businesses who share our same standards and beliefs in environmental and economic sustainability. Our growth is attributed to our fantastic employees, exceptional coffee, and strong underlying belief that what we do can make a difference."

The couple's approach to business has earned both recognition and growth. In the spring of 2014, their 20th year of operation, they were named Maine's Small Business Person of the Year by the U.S. Small Business Administration, judged on staying power, employee growth, and increases in sales. That same year, they opened an expanded roastery with a new café in a 45,000-square-foot Portland warehouse where patrons can observe Lindemann and Spear's devotion to "our mission . . . to preserve the craft of roasting."

"Here at Coffee By Design," the couple say on their business website, "we speak of the many hands that touch our coffee – from farm to cup. . . . We strive to make an extraordinary cup of coffee that people from all walks of life can share and enjoy."

BAXTER
Brewing Co.

In his junior year at Clark University in Worcester, Massachusetts, Luke Livingston began brewing beer in his dormitory room. Later, in 2007, he started an online publication, BlogAboutBeer.com, which he ran for nearly four years – until he sold it in 2009 to plan the launch of a brewery in Lewiston, Maine.

It would be New England's sole craft brewery producing beer only in cans – not bottles – enabling him to make more beer at a lower cost. Cans are better for the environment than glass, better for the beer than glass, more portable than glass, and cheaper than glass, Livingston says.

After raising $1.3 million, he started Baxter Brewing Company at the end of 2010, and shipped his first case of beer in January 2011.

By August of that year, he had doubled the brewery's production with two 60-barrel fermentation tanks and one conditioning tank, bringing start-up costs to $1.4 million. In that first year, the new brewery produced 155,000 gallons of beer and grossed nearly $1 million. In 2012, Livingston added two 20-foot-tall fermentation tanks in an adjacent courtyard and made plans for renovating an 8,000-square-foot warehouse down the street. Expansion continued in the following years.

Having grown up in adjacent Auburn, Livingston liked the idea of revitalizing one of Lewiston's iconic but dormant textile mills, the Bates Mill Complex, as a brewery. "There is a palpable cultural renaissance happening in this community right now," he said then, "and it's a really exciting time to play such a significant role in that revolution.

But more than that, Livingston is driven by the concept of "corporate sustainability."

He defines the term as "a company's responsibility to do as much as it is able –financially, logistically, et cetera – to reduce its negative impact on the environment and the world around us. If a company can go beyond that to better the environment and maybe even look at sustainability as a source of secondary revenue, as many breweries including Baxter do, then they're all the better for it.

"But at its core, corporate sustainability, to me as a business owner, is all about trying to have the least amount of negative impact on our world as I can."

Phil Coupe had an idea: Maine should reduce its reliance on fossil fuels and its creation of carbon dioxide. He and a couple of like-minded visionaries, Fortunat Mueller and Bill Behrens, began exploring how to do it. In 2003, they started a little company, which they named ReVision Energy, in hopes of launching an energy revolution in Maine.

It turned out to be a practical, workable idea.

Within a decade, ReVision Energy had grown from four employees to 45, at three locations in Maine and another in New Hampshire, earning $7.9 million while installing 3,000 solar electricity and hot water systems and Maine's first solar power charging stations for electric vehicles.

People – and policymakers – became more aware of the environmental importance of sustainable energy, but not of its costs. "There's still a fair amount of ignorance about the cost-effectiveness of renewable energy and what it can and cannot do," Coupe told *Mainebiz* magazine in 2012. "We look at our efforts in Augusta as trying to help people understand the opportunity that renewable energy represents for the state. It's not about making ReVision a big or wealthy company, it's about solving the state's energy problems."

With its heavy reliance on fossil fuels, Coupe estimates that Maine sends $5 billion out of the state every year. Converting to solar, wind, tidal, and other renewable energy sources such as wood pellets, he believes, would keep that money in Maine, spurring long-term economic growth and making the state less reliant on things beyond its control.

Still, for many people who might like the concept of solar panels on their roofs, spending money today to save money in the future can be difficult. But renewable power costs are steadily dropping, Coupe and Mueller say, while fossil fuel costs are not.

They and the company's third founding partner, Behrens, set their sights on building ReVision as the New England's top solar installation company while sparking Maine's energy revolution. With Behrens heading ReVision's photovoltaic division and managing its finances, the enterprise was making good progress in 2015.

Several Maine communities began launching "Solarize" programs, through which residential and commercial energy users jointly buy solar energy equipment at a reduced cost through municipal bulk purchases. Townspeople in Brunswick, for example, voted in 2015 to have ReVision sell and install their solar energy equipment, and residents of several other Maine communities have done the same.

"We're really riding the beginning of a wave," Coupe said, "that I think is going to change the way we use energy across Maine and hopefully across the country."

PUTNEY
Committed to Quality. Delivering Affordability.

Jean Hoffman's aging cat Dude had become very thin. A veterinarian told her Dude was suffering from hyperthyroidism, and prescribed a daily medication that in 2000 was available only as an expensive, branded drug in doses intended for humans. Hoffman could afford it, but she wondered: Why was there no generic version for pets?

Hoffman, who has a background in pharmaceutical management, soon learned that although generic drugs accounted for more than 80 percent of human prescriptions filled in the United States – at a savings of $3 billion every week for American consumers – only 7 percent of drugs for pets had generic equivalents.

So six years later, she combined her love of pets with her industry savvy to launch Putney, Inc., a Portland company that develops generic equivalents for branded pet medications for which veterinarians have identified demand. The company contracts with research and development firms for the research and, after it receives a patent, contracts with drug manufacturers to make the medications in facilities that are compliant with US Food and Drug Administration regulations. Keeping overhead low allows for quick responses to market demands.

Still, Hoffman says, "It's a long, expensive, and scientifically difficult process to develop the drugs and get them through the FDA review process."

Since launching her company, she told an interviewer a few years later, Putney, Inc., brought five generic pet medications to market, with more than 20 additional products awaiting FDA approval. When they receive it and go into distribution, Hoffman expects the company's annual revenue will hit the $100 million mark.

"We believe we have the deepest pipeline in veterinary medicine," Hoffman added, "aimed at providing veterinarians and pet owners with FDA-approved generics of pet medicines where price is a barrier to prescribing and using the right drug for each pet's medical need.

"This is one of the few opportunities in the pharmaceutical industry – a worldwide business – to build a company of scale doing the right thing and making a lot of money in a way that serves the customer," she says.

Shopping for groceries on a cold February day in 2004, lifelong New Englander and veteran entrepreneur Paul Sellew looked at the supermarket displays of tomatoes from Canada, Holland, and Mexico and thought: "Wouldn't it be great to grow fully vine-ripened greenhouse tomatoes right here at home? Shipping distances would be shorter, and there would be better taste because the tomatoes could be more fully ripened before moving them to market."

One year later in Madison, Maine, where electric lighting costs are low, he launched Backyard Farms on a former dairy farm. Sellew, whose family runs a large wholesale nursery in Connecticut, recruited Dutch-born Arie Vandergiessen, a leading greenhouse grower, and Wayne Davis, a former executive with Fidelity Investments, to help develop the project.

The venture became operational in 2006, with a huge, 25-acre hydroponic greenhouse growing vine-ripened tomatoes year-round for delivery to New England grocery stores the day after they're picked. Three years later, a second greenhouse was built, connected to the first, expanding total capacity to 42 glass-covered acres, irrigated with rain water from the roof and pollinated by 48,000 bumblebees that live inside. Eleven thousand specialized 1,000-watt lights, controlled by computer, mimic what the sun would provide under ideal conditions for year-round photosynthesis. By 2014, the vast indoor farm employed about 200 gardeners and other workers.

Mostly owned by Boston-based Devonshire Investments, a branch of Fidelity Investments, the farm grows 27 million pounds of tomatoes year-round, as New England's premium tomato producer, delivering to about 30 retailers, from Wal-Mart to Hannaford to Whole Foods.

Backyard Farms grew through a succession of chief executives. Late in 2007, Sellew ceded his CEO title and day-to-day oversight of the company to Roy Lubetkin, a former president of a division of Agway Inc. Lubetkin, in turn, was replaced in 2011 by Chuck Green, who previously had led and managed several food industry companies. Green left in 2013 to become a business consultant, declaring on his LinkedIn page that he had instituted changes "resulting in company profits for the first time in almost a decade." In mid-2014, a former Dole Food Co. vice president of operations, Stuart Jablon, was named to head the company.

As a young Army officer supervising communication networks and information technology systems, Josh Broder "was in 22 countries in 4½ years, building and managing systems in Afghanistan, Uzbekistan, Pakistan – all over," he later told a Maine magazine. "It really accelerated my interest in leadership and management."

In 2006, he arrived at Tilson Technology Management, a Portland telecommunications and information technology consulting firm that focused on construction projects.

When Broder's mentor, Chief Executive Officer Mike Dow, left during the Great Recession in 2009 to pursue international interests, Broder took over and began reinventing the company. "We decided to focus on things that were moving in the economy, and that was government," he told a Maine magazine. The American Recovery and Reinvestment Act, he added, "really fueled our growth."

He drove Tilson's revenues from $4 million in 2010 to $7 million in 2011 and $14 million in 2012, leading several large, successful Recovery Act-funded technology infrastructure projects in New England. The company grew from fewer than 10 employees to more than 100 while building telecommunications networks, erecting cell towers and laying fiber.

By 2015, Tilson was operating in two fast-growing and service capacity-constrained markets: telecommunications facilities development for cellular, smart grid and government; and consulting, software development, and information systems deployment specializing in construction applications.

Recognized for its sustained high growth and profitability, Tilson was on Inc. Magazine's list of the 5,000 fastest-growing private US companies from 2011 through 2014. By 2015, Tilson had offices developing and installing technology software and hardware in New York, New Jersey, Alabama, and Colorado.

In Maine, Tilson led the construction and management of the state's 1,100-mile Three Ring Binder broadband project, a $32 million expansion of the state's broadband network to connect underserved parts of the state. The company did similar work in central and western Massachusetts with an $80 million project.

"We try to take a holistic approach and balance all those interests," Broder said at the time. "They can be particularly complicated when you're dealing with political and policy aspects. Government projects often have built-in controversy and challenges."

In 2015, Broder predicted that government work would slow as budget constraints squeeze spending, but private work would increase, especially in industries with strong ties to the creative economy. "American centers of innovation are our capital – the companies coming from technology, software, and social media," he said. "All of those new things require significant infrastructure – and we're the infrastructure provider."

THE NEWEST WAVE OF EMERGING INNOVATORS

The highest tides in the world are in the Bay of Fundy, bounded by Nova Scotia, New Brunswick, and northeastern Maine. In the continental United States, no tides are higher than those striking the Maine island town of Eastport, and it is here that Chris Sauer launched his vision of turning tides into electricity.

After earning a bachelor's degree in civil engineering from the University of Illinois in 1969, Sauer began a career as an innovative entrepreneur in successful engineering ventures. He cofounded Ocean Renewable Power Company in Portland five years later as its chief technology officer, spearheading development of North America's first tidal-power turbine. Two years later, he became the company's president and chief executive officer.

And in 2013, Ocean Renewable installed a 100-foot-long turbine generator 60 feet below the surface of Cobscook Bay, on the west side of Eastport. It looked something like a gigantic version of the blades of a hand-powered lawnmower and could produce 180 kilowatts, enough electricity for 25 homes. Although that is less than the possible output of a typical wind turbine, tidal current never stops. "When the wind blows, you get electricity," Sauer says, "but you don't know when that's going to be."

The US Department of Energy provided $10 million of the turbine generator's roughly $21 million cost.

The following year, in 2014, Ocean Renewable built a smaller turbine generator in an Alaskan river, providing power to a village of 70 people who had been relying on costly diesel generators for their electricity. State and federal energy agencies provided $1.5 million of the cost, and Ocean Renewable invested about $2 million.

The projects are complex undertakings, with government involvement to address environmental protection considerations and financial support, commercial viability, and extensive, ongoing research and testing to refine and improve the turbine generators.

The company's website notes that "every ORPC project is carried out in collaboration with local communities, universities, environmental agencies, fishing industry groups, and other major stakeholders. ORPC's Maine Tidal Energy Project has already brought more than $25 million into the state economy, and has created or helped retain more than 100 jobs in 14 Maine counties. These same benefits will be realized in Alaska and Nova Scotia, where we are also actively working with local groups to make tidal and river energy a reality."

In the future, the company says, it "will be forging new strategic and financial partnerships that will allow us to expand our operations in North America, and eventually offer our technology and expertise to ocean and river energy projects worldwide."

In the best entrepreneurial tradition, Shannon Kinney started her online marketing agency, Dream Local Digital, in her midcoast Maine garage in early 2009, after two decades of national advertising experience.

She envisioned an enterprise that would expand media partnerships and develop new product offerings to adapt and lead the way in the ever-changing media advertising, social media, and digital marketing industries.

A stuffed honey badger, a bit like a teddy bear with a blue cape emblazoned with the company's name, is on display in Dream Local's Rockland offices as an inspiration to employees to pursue agency goals with relentless passion. "The honey badger ties our corporate culture together," she explains: "the dedication and the drive, the willingness to do whatever needs to be done to get the job done." And although she is her company's chief executive, Kinney calls herself the "client success officer," reflecting her focus on satisfying customers.

Noting that "the Internet has changed the way people make buying decisions," Kinney says Dream Local Digital guides small and medium-sized businesses, as well as newspapers, media companies, and ad agencies, in using social media marketing to increase sales to both new and existing customers. The agency's online marketing ranges from website development, content strategy, and social media to search engine optimization, reputation management, and e-mail marketing.

On its website, the company tells prospective clients that *"We manage your online marketing so you can manage your business. We can maintain your clients' social media channels, giving them the ability to focus on their own work and allowing you to retain customers by offering a wider range of advertising options."*

Living and working as an assistant chef in New York City, Mike St. Pierre loved his occasional opportunities to get away on weekend backpacking hikes. When he wasn't on a mountain trail, he was focusing on how to make his hiking gear lighter. By 2008, he was researching backpacking equipment with an eye toward making his own. "I started to really think about what I was putting into my pack," he recalled a couple of years later. "I began weighing my gear and building spread sheets to help organize everything."

That's how Hyperlite Mountain Gear was born. It began with a simple, tarp-like tent, and a minimalist, waterproof backpack that weighed just a pound and a half. With high-tech fabrics, these first products were ultra-strong as well as ultra-light. "Lighter and stronger? How can it not catch on?" St. Pierre wondered. "Anyone who has tried it will admit that it is so much more comfortable being fully and safely equipped with 15 pounds of gear instead of 40 to 50 pounds."

By then, he and his co-founder brother, Dan St. Pierre, a Wharton School of Business graduate with 20 years of experience in corporate finance and entrepreneurship, had launched their manufacturing shop in borrowed basement space.

Within a couple of years, though, the fledgling company had moved into 1,000 square feet of space in a turn-of-the-century textile mill in Biddeford.

In 2014, the company raised $908,000 in equity financing and a bank loan to support new investment in marketing, product development and staff. Venture funds and private investors provided equity capital, and a local savings bank provided debt.

By mid-year, Hyperlite had moved into 7,500 square feet of nearby space in the renovated Pepperell Mill Campus, producing expensive but highly regarded backpacks, shelters, stuff packs, and accessories. "We've brought manufacturing back to a place where American workers were manufacturing more than century ago," St. Pierre said. "I'm proud of that."

He told a magazine interviewer that "it's been really rewarding to create new jobs in these difficult economic times, especially in manufacturing, a sector that has been in decline in the USA for many years. Manufacturing at home also allows us to keep a very close eye on quality control, and it allows us to be nimble when it comes to design changes and product development."

Double Blue
Sports Analytics

In the summer of 2013, Dan Kerluke had an idea that prompted him to give up his job as a University of Maine hockey coach: a new and better way for hockey goalies and goaltending coaches to record and analyze goalie performance data, with an Apple iPad application.

But the iPad app existed only in Kerluke's imagination, and that of the Black Bears' part-time goaltending coach, David Alexander. It would need a lot of work. By the end of that year, though, the two ex-hockey coaches and computer programmer Tim Westbaker had founded a company, Double Blue Sports Analytics, and launched what they named the 360 Save Review System app.

"It's great to have an idea for an app, but you have to build it, too," Kerluke told a newspaper interviewer. "That's the hardest part. Without Tim, this wouldn't have been possible." The app also had beta testers: goaltending coaches for two NHL teams, the Dallas Stars and New Jersey Devils.

As the first company to offer a goalie-specific data analysis product, Double Blue made its 360 Save Review System available on Apple's App Store early in 2014 with a $300 annual subscription, and it soon drew hundreds of users.

The app works with a GoPro video camera recording of each period, from puck drop to buzzer. After a game, the camera's video is uploaded to an iPad for the app's statistical analytics. The process – which typically takes a player or goalie coach hours to compile, edit, arrange and analyze without the app – takes only a few minutes, with advanced video and statistical analytics.

After raising nearly $250,000 in start-up capital – mostly from family and friends, and the Maine Technology Institute – the Orono start-up company grew to four employees and began plans to expand. Kerluke foresaw a potential suite of potential related apps to help hockey coaches capture and analyze performance data for an entire roster, ranging from a center winning a face-off to players taking shots. And he soon realized that Double Blue's technology could be adapted to other sports.

After practicing medicine in rural Maine for two decades, Dr. Daniel Mingle had grown increasingly dissatisfied with the quality of service that physicians were able to provide. The problem, he saw, was the difficulty doctors had in sharing medical information with each other about their patients. In 1998, he had an opportunity to do something about it. He closed his medical office and began developing an electronic medical records system at MaineGeneral Medical Center in Augusta.

As head of the hospital's technology department, Mingle built a way for doctors to do more than share medical information. His system also provided weekly reports to each physician practice detailing its performance against key measures and alerts indicating best treatment practices. But it took time to convince doctors to use the system. Initially, the reports electronically delivered to physician offices were ignored, and doctors often had one reaction to sharing a patient's chart, Mingle said at the time: "It's a great idea, but it will never work."

But more and more doctors discovered that it did work, and came to rely on it. And so Mingle made a pivotal decision to launch his own electronic medical records enterprise. In South Paris, he started Mingle Analytics LLC, a "health care informatics and strategic consulting company."

The Maine Center for Entrepreneurial Development, a nonprofit resource in Portland that helps promising entrepreneurs to grow through innovation, provided crucial start-up help to Mingle Analytics. The center describes itself as "helping entrepreneurs re-invent the Maine economy by providing them with resources to build innovative world-class companies." It has what it calls a "Top Gun Track," which accelerates "entrepreneurial development using training, mentoring and the development of community connections."

Dr. Mingle qualified for the center's Top Gun program, which helped him focus and stabilize his fledgling company's growth. Ten years ago, he remarked to a Maine magazine in 2014, he would not have predicted he'd start a new company. "It was never my intention to open a new business," he said. But having opened one, he added, "I'm not working with the goal to retire."

 **John Lovell** was for three decades a Maine newspaper reporter and editor at the *Portland Press Herald* and the *Falmouth Forecaster*, as well as The Associated Press, and later, the editor of several Maine magazines, including *Port City Life*, *Habitat* (published by Maine Audubon), and the *Maine Bar Journal* (published by the Maine State Bar Association). During many of his newspaper years he was also an adjunct professor of journalism at the University of Southern Maine. His freelance magazine writing has been published in the *Boston Globe Sunday Magazine*, *Newsweek*, *Sports Afield*, *Parade Magazine*, *Yankee Magazine*, *DownEast* Magazine and other publications. Nationally accredited in public relations, he has also provided strategic public relations planning and marketing communications services to corporations, law firms, associations, state agencies, and political campaigns. He lives in Portland, providing freelance writing, editing, and public relations services to various corporate and organization clients. His email address is jmlovell@gmail.com.

Made in the USA
San Bernardino, CA
23 November 2015